THE LOUISIANA PROUD COLLECTION OF
HOME COOKING

LOUISIANA

PROUD

D1411037

**Compiled and Illustrated by
ANDY SMITH**

**Edited by
ANDREW M. SMITH, SR.**

A LOUISIANA PROUD PRESS BOOK

A Louisiana Proud Press Book
Copyright ©1991 by Andy Smith
All rights reserved including the right of reproduction
in whole or in part in any form.
Published by Louisiana Proud Press
Edited by Andrew M. Smith, Sr.
Printed by Baton Rouge Printing Company
Page composition by Advanced Consulting Group
International Standard Book Number 0-9618564-3-2

Louisiana Proud is registered and copyrighted and is not to be used or
reproduced in any manner without written permission by the author. All
recipes and illustrations are copyrighted and are not be reproduced in
any manner with out the permission of Louisiana Proud Press or the
original donor.

For Information Contact:
Louisiana Proud
6133 Goodwood Ave
Baton Rouge, Louisiana 70806

Dedicated to all the cooks in all the towns of Louisiana, especially to the 276 Louisianians who made this book by sharing one of their recipes with us.

SPECIAL THANKS

Jane P. Ogea

Truly this project would not have been completed without the overall assistance provided by Jane. She went on trips to give out recipe forms, typed some when they came in, and took photos of towns not already drawn. She worked with the production of the pages by proofing, cutting and shooting of the art work.

Mrs. Evelyn Duke

Mrs. Duke, a retired home economist who lives in Columbia in Caldwell Parish, was instrumental in the planning of the project. She was firm in the belief that we should get a recipe from a person who lives in each of the individual towns. This became the major theme and the motivating factor. Mrs. Duke also called upon some forty of her friends and fellow home economists to provide recipes.

Joy, Eileen and Nanette Sonnier

Three good friends who also called upon people they came in contact with in their businesses, along with their good friends who lived in different towns. Their efforts also provided about forty recipes from the Lafayette and New Orleans areas.

THE LOUISIANA PROUD COLLECTION

This Collection which started in 1982 now consists of over 1600 illustrations and 18,000 photographs. It is an ongoing project which focuses on the towns and the buildings of the State. All the drawings used are taken from the Louisiana Proud Collection. The Collection has been used to produce three volumes of towns and their histories. Each town represented in the series consists of 5 drawings and a brief historical sketch of it. The Collection is an attempt to record what the State really looks like, as the cookbook shows what the flavors of Louisiana are.

In order to obtain these photographs the entire State was crisscrossed many times. One part of the discovery of the State is observing the different faces of the landscape. Another is sampling the different tastes of the State. Out of the traveling and tasting came the idea for the cookbook. Even though Louisiana's reputation for food has grown internationally most of the cookbooks remain either sectional or specialized in nature.

What do people really eat? What do they cook for their families? THE LOUISIANA PROUD COLLECTION OF HOME COOKING presents a look and taste of the entire State. Two hundred seventy six people, all from different towns, gave us a recipe. Each page contains one recipe, an illustration of a building in that town and the contributor's name. The resulting cookbook is truly a sampling of all the tastes of Louisiana.

HOW RECIPES WERE OBTAINED

"We would appreciate your help in obtaining a recipe from your town. This should be a recipe that your family likes. The cookbook will be entitled HOME COOKING. We would like the recipe to be something that can be prepared without a whole lot of special ingredients. The best test would probably be just 'something good'.

We want to create a cookbook that features meals that are cooked throughout the entire state. This is not intended to be a regional cookbook. It is a Louisiana cookbook. A LOUISIANA PROUD COOKBOOK."

A cookbook that gives the real flavor of the state was the goal. In order to accomplish this individuals who actually lived in the towns represented were contacted and asked to submit ONE recipe. "Something you cook for the family." Something that didn't require lots of special ingredients. Something that could be prepared from ingredients on your shelf or from the freezer.

A form was prepared with the above instructions and the people were contacted. Some were contacted by mail, some alerted first by phone and then sent a form but most were contacted personally. Armed with a bunch of forms we went from town to town and literally just dropped in. Most everyone contacted complied with the strange request from someone they had never met. The result is a cookbook truly representative of the State.

There was no instruction on what to send in. It could be in any category. A few of the recipes were the same but usually from a different section of the State, however, they were usually different in ingredients and preparation.

TABLE OF CONTENTS

HOW THE BOOK IS DIVIDED

A note about the layout of the book will make it easier to find a specific town. As in the Louisiana Proud Book Series, the Cookbook is broken into 5 sections. These sections relate to the geographical sections of the state, Southeast, Southwest, etc.

The Table of Contents will bring you to the start of each section. There you will find an alphabetical listing of each town represented and a map of the section you are about to enter. The towns are in alphabetical order until you reach the next section.

There are also indexes by town and one by recipe category in the back of the book.

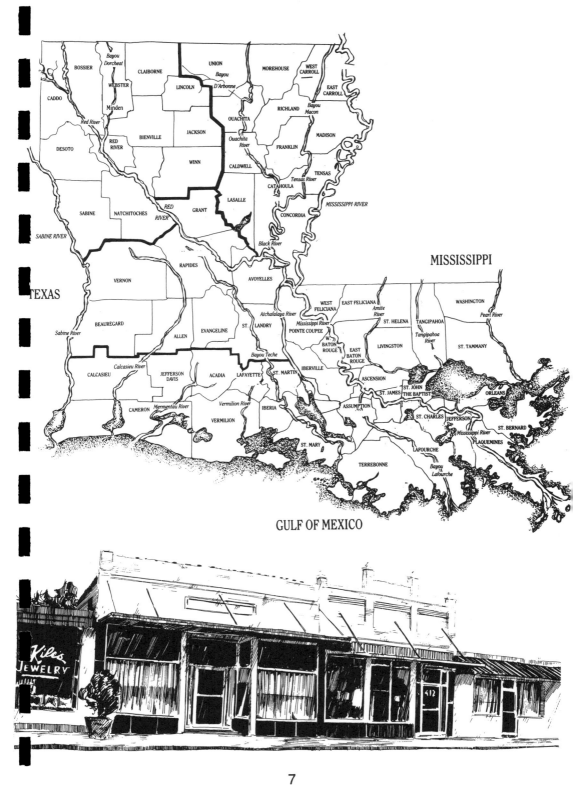

GULF OF MEXICO

MISSISSIPPI

TEXAS

7

Southeast Section

Abita Springs
Addis
Albany
Algiers
Amite
Angie
Arabie
Baker
Baton Rouge
Bogalusa
Bourg
Brusly
Buras
Chalmette
Clinton
Cocodrie
Convent
Covington
Cut Off
Denham Springs
Des Allemands
Destrahan
Donaldsonville
Edgard
Erwinville
Ethel
Folsom
Franklinton
French Settlement
Galliano
Garyville
Geismar
Gibson
Golden Meadow
Gonzales
Gramercy
Greensburg

Gretna
Hahnville
Hammond
Harvey
Houma
Independence
Jackson
Kentwood
LaPlace
Labadieville
Livingston
Livonia
Lockport
Luling
Lutcher
Madisonville
Mandeville
Maringouin
Maurepas
Metairie
Montegut
Morganza
Napoleonville
New Orleans
New Roads
Norco
Norwood
Paincourtville
Paradis
Pierre Part
Plains
Plaquemine

Point A La Hache
Ponchatoula
Port Allen
Port Sulphur
Port Vincent
Prairieville
Raceland
Reserve
Rosedale
Slaughter
Slidell
Sorrento
St. Francisville
St Gabriel
Thibodaux
Tickfaw
Vacherie
Varnado
Violet
Westwego
White Castle
Whitehall
Wilson
Zachary

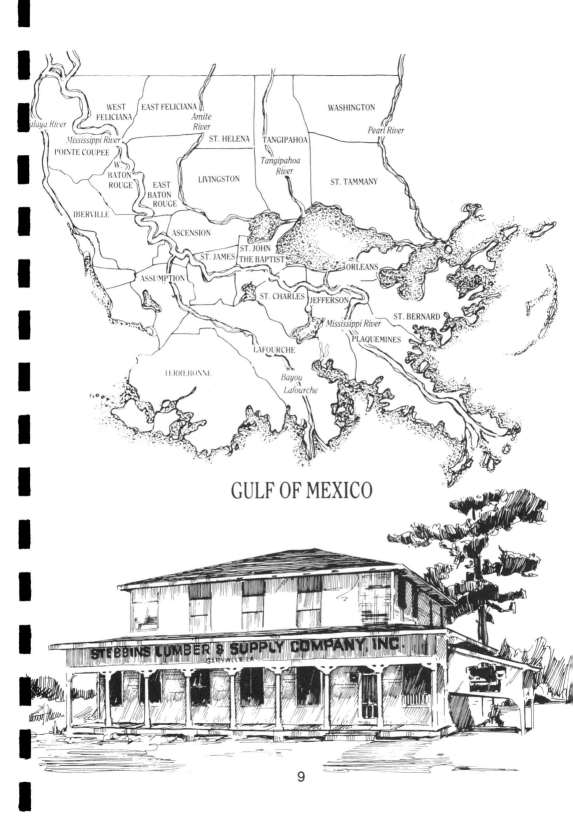

GULF OF MEXICO

Stewed Chicken
SERVES 4-6

4 to 5 lb. stewing chicken, cut in serving pieces
5 tbsp. flour
1/2 cup cooking oil
1 large onion, chopped
2 cups celery, chopped
2 tbsp. bell pepper, chopped
3 tbsp. green onions, chopped
2 tbsp. parsley, chopped
1 tbsp. garlic, mashed
13 oz. can button mushrooms
1 bay leaf
1 small sprig thyme
Salt and pepper to taste
6 cups hot water

Wash and trim fat from chicken, salt and pepper and brown in oil in heavy iron pot. Remove chicken and set aside. Make roux in drippings. Add onions, garlic, bell pepper and celery. When seasonings are clear add 6 cups of hot water and return chicken to pot. Add bay leaf and thyme. Cook 1 1/2 hours or until chicken is tender and gravy has thickened. Add mushrooms before serving. Serve over cooked rice. Enjoy!

ABITA SPRINGS
Sue Wolfe
ST. TAMMANY PARISH

Lazy Man's Meat Loaf
SERVES 4 -6

1 lb. ground meat
1/2 tsp. garlic, diced
2 tbsp. dried onion
1 tbsp. dried parsley
1 tbsp. dried bell pepper
1/2 cup milk
1/2 cup Italian bread crumbs
1/2 tsp. salt
1/4 tsp. red pepper
1 egg
Dash of Lea and Perrin
1 can Rotel tomatoes
1 large or 2 small cans Dawn Fresh Mushroom sauce

Shape all ingredients into a loaf and put into a casserole dish.
Add 1 can Rotel tomatoes and 1 large or 2 cans of Dawn Fresh
mushroom sauce. Bake at 350 degrees for 1 hour. Very
moist and delicious.

ADDIS

Joy A. Tullier
WEST BATON ROUGE PARISH

11

Pork And Bean Surprise
SERVES 6

1 large can pork and beans
3 tbsp. brown sugar
1 tbsp. barbecue sauce
1 lb. ground meat
Salt and pepper to taste

Brown meat and drain. Sprinkle 3 tbsp. brown sugar, and 1 tbsp. barbecue sauce. Add 1 large can pork and beans, add salt and pepper, cover and let simmer 10 to 15 minutes.

ALBANY
Sammie Clardy
LIVINGSTON PARISH

Chicken Parmesan
SERVES 4

4 boneless chicken breasts
1/4 cup olive oil
2 tbsp. Worcestershire
1/2 cup bread crumbs
2 cans tomato sauce
2 tsp. basil
1 egg, beaten
1/4 stick butter
1/2 cup Parmesan cheese
Provolone or Mozzarella cheese (sliced)
Angel Hair pasta

Using a mallet, flatten breasts to 1/2 inch thickness. Dip each breast in the beaten egg. Lightly coat each breast with bread crumbs. Brown in olive oil and transfer to baking dish. In a sauce pan, combine tomato sauce, Worcestershire sauce, butter and basil. Simmer for 20 minutes. Pour over chicken. Sprinkle with Parmesan cheese and bake covered at 325 degrees for 45 minutes. Remove cover and top each breast with the Provolone or Mozzarella cheese. Serve with Angel Hair pasta lightly tossed with butter and fresh basil.

ALGIERS

Keith Jordan
ORLEANS PARISH

Oyster Rockefeller Casserole
SERVES 6

2 sticks butter or oleo
3/4 cup bread crumbs
3 boxes chopped spinach
1/2 tsp. thyme
2 to 3 dozen oysters, drained
1 tbsp. anise flavored liquor (Absinthe)
1/2 cup green onions, chopped fine
1/4 cup fresh parsley, chopped
Salt, black pepper, white pepper and red pepper to taste

Melt butter; add thyme and green onions. Saute' for about
two minutes. Add bread crumbs and saute' until crumbs are
toasted. Add drained oysters and simmer until oysters curl up
on edges. Add parsley. Add liquor (Absinthe, Pernod or
Herbsaint) to oyster mixture. Cook frozen spinach according
to directions; drain well. Add to oyster mixture, mix well. Bake
for 20 to 25 minutes in 425 degree oven. Season to taste.
May be served in oyster shells or individual servings or can be
used as dip with Melba Toast. (NOTE: If liquor is unavailable,
boil 1 1/2 tbsp. anise seed in 1/2 cup water for 10 minutes,
strain, then use liquid.)

AMITE

Ruth Gillen
TANGIPAHOA PARISH

Blueberry Pound Cake

SERVES 12

1 cup butter, softened
2 cups sugar
4 eggs
1 tsp. vanilla
3 cups plain flour, divided
1/2 tsp. salt
1 tsp. baking powder
2 cups fresh or frozen blueberries

Cream butter and sugar. Add eggs one at a time and beat until light and fluffy. Add vanilla. Sift 2 cups flour, salt and baking powder together. Add sifted ingredients to creamed mixture and beat. Dredge berries in remaining flour. Fold mixture gently into creamed mixture. Pour mixture into a tube pan which has been buttered and coated with sugar. Bake in preheated oven at 325 degrees for 1 hour and 15 minutes.

ANGIE

Sally Fornea

WASHINGTON PARISH

Crab Soup
SERVES 4

1 stick butter
1 small onion, chopped
1 can cream of celery soup
1 pint Half and Half
1 lb. fresh or frozen crabmeat

Saute' onion in butter. Add crabmeat and cream of celery soup. Add Half and Half.

ARABI
Judy Roy
ST. BERNARD PARISH

Macaroni And Cheese Casserole
SERVES 5

1 can tomato paste
1 can tomato sauce
1/2 large onion, chopped
2 bell peppers, chopped
1 box Kraft Macaroni and Cheese
1 lb. ground chuck
3 cups water
Salt and black pepper to taste

Brown the ground chuck in a medium sized cooking pot, drain excess fat. Add onion, bell pepper, salt and black pepper, cook for 2 to 3 minutes. Add tomato paste, tomato sauce and water. Let simmer 15 to 20 minutes. Prepare macaroni and cheese (follow instructions on box). Add macaroni and cheese to the simmered pot, place all ingredients into a casserole dish and bake at 350 degrees for 20 minutes.

BAKER
Kim McConkey
EAST BATON ROUGE PARISH

Fish And Broccoli Roll-ups
SERVES 4-5

8 to 10 fillets of trout
1/2 bunch broccoli
1 can cream of celery soup
1/2 can white wine
1 bunch green onions, sliced lengthwise
Parmesan cheese
Salt and pepper to taste

Cut broccoli with some stem left on and slice onions. Boil
about 5 minutes. Put broccoli and green onions on fish. Roll
up and put tooth pick to hold them. Put in casserole. Mix soup
and wine and pour over the rolled up fish. Cover with
Parmesan cheese. Bake at 350 degrees for 30 minutes.

BATON ROUGE
Audrey Smith
EAST BATON ROUGE PARISH

Slush Punch
SERVES 75

2 46 oz. cans Dole pineapple juice
1 large can frozen orange juice
1/2 cup Real Lemon juice
2 40 oz. bottles white grape juice
1 oz. almond extract
2 large boxes lemon Jello
1 1/2 gallons of water

Combine all ingredients except Jello. Make a simple syrup of
5 cups sugar and 4 cups water. When the syrup boils,
remove from heat and add Jello. Stir well. Add to fruit juice.
Freeze in gallon containers. Remove from freezer 3 hours
before serving. Thaw to slush consistency. Favorite recipe for
bridal tea shower or wedding reception.

BOGALUSA
Shirley Saltaformaggio
WASHINGTON PARISH

Tina's Cajun Country Cabbage Rolls

SERVES 10-12

1 large head fresh green cabbage
1 1/2 lb. ground meat (may substitute pork)
3/4 cup raw rice
1 tbsp. bell pepper, minced
1 tbsp. celery, minced
1 tbsp. parsley, minced
1/2 small onion, minced
1 egg
1 small can tomato sauce
Salt and pepper to taste

Heat a large pot of boiling water and drop in cabbage
leaves. Let stand about 5 minutes (until wilted). Remove,
drain and set aside to cool while mixing stuffing. Place meat
in mixing bowl with salt and pepper. Add rice, bell pepper,
celery, parsley, onion and 1/2 can tomato sauce. Mix
thoroughly. Place 1 heaping tbsp. of stuffing on edge of large
wilted leaf. Fold sides and roll up tightly. Place close together
into a large sauce pan. Keep making rolls until you run out of
mixture. Pour remaining tomato sauce on top of rolls and add
water to cover rolls. Place left over leaves to form a blanket to
cover rolls and add salt and pepper. Allow to simmer over direct
heat for about 1 hour or until rice is cooked. Serve hot.

BOURG
Tina Freeman
TERREBONNE PARISH

Rosemary's Pecan Pie
SERVES 6

2 eggs, slightly beaten
1 cup sugar
1 cup corn syrup
1 9" uncooked pie shell
1 tsp. vanilla extract
1 cup pecan nuts, chopped

Combine eggs, sugar, corn syrup and vanilla to create filling.
Sprinkle nuts in unbaked shell and add filling. Bake in hot 450
degree oven for 10 minutes. Turn oven down to 325 degrees
and bake for 60 minutes or until mixture does not adhere to a
knife. Bake on sheet of foil as filling tends to run over.

BRUSLY
Rosemary L. Bernard
WEST BATON ROUGE PARISH

Shrimp And Sausage Jambalaya
SERVES 6-8

1 quart cleaned raw shrimp
3 large onions, chopped
1 large bell pepper, chopped
1/2 cup parsley, chopped
4 tbsp. flour
1/2 cup oil
3 cups cooked rice
2 lbs. sausage
Garlic powder to taste
Salt and pepper to taste

This is cooked best in iron pot. Brown flour in oil. Add onions,
bell pepper and garlic and cook until tender. Add shrimp and
cut up sausage (cut in cubes). Cook until done. Add water to
make thick gravy. Add parsley and simmer. Boil rice until
cooked then drain. Fold rice into gravy and let set until gravy
is absorbed. Salt and pepper to taste. Enjoy.

BURAS HIGH SCHOOL

BURAS
Karen Despeaux Callais
PLAQUEMINES PARISH

Crawfish Dip
SERVES 6-8

2 lbs. crawfish tails, peeled
3/4 cup flour
1 can cream of mushroom soup
1 stick butter
1 medium onion, chopped
1 green pepper, chopped
3 or 4 sticks celery, chopped
3 or 4 green onions, chopped
Salt, black pepper and cayenne pepper to taste

Finely chop all seasonings. Saute' seasonings in butter. Add all the other ingredients in the following order: Stir in flour, the mushroom soup (at this point make sure there are no lumps of flour in mixture). Add peeled crawfish tails, salt, black and cayenne pepper to taste. Serve warm with your favorite chips or crackers.

CHALMETTE
Edward Lovell
ST. BERNARD PARISH

23

Quick Peach Cobbler
SERVES 6

1/2 cup butter or margarine
1 cup self-rising flour
2 cups sugar, divided
1 cup milk
4 cups peaches, sliced

Combine peaches and 1 cup sugar, bring to a boil. Melt butter in 13" X 9" X 2" pan. Combine flour, 1 cup sugar and milk. Mix well, pour over melted butter (do not stir). Pour peach and sugar mixture over batter. Bake in 350 degree oven for 30 minutes.

CLINTON
Evelyn P. Beauchamp
EAST FELICIANA PARISH

Old Time Seashore Oyster Or Shrimp Jambalaya
SERVES 4

1 pint oysters or shrimp
1 large onions or 2 medium onions, chopped
1 1/2 lbs. sliced salt meat
1 3/4 cup long grain rice
Salt and pepper to taste

Brown salt meat and chopped onions. This gives color and flavor. Make as dark as you desire. Boil salt meat 8 to 10 minutes. Reserve liquid. Cut salt meat in 1 inch squares. Add oysters or shrimp. Season to taste. (You can add some salt meat water). Add enough water to cook rice. Add rice. Cook on low fire until done.

COCODRIE

Vivian V. Vincent/Caliste Hebert
TERREBONNE PARISH

Crawfish Fettucine

SERVES 12

3 sticks butter
3 medium onions, chopped
3 ribs celery, chopped
2 bell peppers, chopped
1/4 cup flour
4 tbsp. parsley, chopped
3 lbs. crawfish tails, peeled
1 quart Half and Half

1 lb. Velveeta cheese, 1/2 in. cubes
2 tbsp. jalapeno peppers, chopped
3 cloves garlic, crushed
1 lb. packaged fettucine noodles
Salt and pepper to taste
Parmesan cheese to taste

Melt butter in large heavy saucepan. Add onions, celery and bell peppers. Cook 10 minutes until clear. Add flour, blend in well. Cover and cook 15 minutes, stirring occasionally. Add parsley and crawfish tails. Cover and cook 20 minutes, stirring often. Add cream, cheese, jalapenos and garlic. Mix well. Add salt and pepper to taste. Cook covered on low heat 20 minutes, stirring occasionally. Cook noodles according to package directions. Drain and add sauce. Mix thoroughly. Pour into 3 quart buttered casserole dish. Sprinkle with Parmesan cheese. Bake at 350 degrees for 12 minutes.

CONVENT

Terry S. Louque
ST. JAMES PARISH

26

Marinated Shrimp, Mushrooms and Artichoke Hearts

(SERVES SEVERAL)

2-3 lbs. fresh shrimp, peeled and cooked
2 4 oz. cans whole button mushrooms, drained
2 14 oz. cans tiny artichoke hearts, drained
2-3 onions, sliced thinly and ringed
1 bottle capers, drained
1 package Good Seasons Blue Cheese salad dressing
1 package Good Seasons Italian salad dressing
1 package Good Seasons Cheese and Garlic salad dressing
1/2 tsp. salt

Prepare dressings according to package directions, omitting water and replacing with vinegar. Put all ingredients in a deep bowl and marinate over night. This must be stirred occasionally and very carefully to avoid breaking up artichoke hearts.

COVINGTON

Bunt Percy
ST. TAMMANY PARISH

Shrimp Salad

SERVES 6

8 oz. bag macaroni spirals
1 1/2 cups boiled shrimp
3 hard boiled eggs
8-12 pimento olives, diced
2-3 sweet pickles, diced
1/2 cup celery, dice
1/3 cup bell peppers, diced
1 tbsp. mustard
1/2 cup mayonnaise
Salt
Pepper
Paprika

Boil macaroni and let cool. Mash egg yolks with 1 tbsp. mustard and 1/2 cup mayonnaise (use more if you have increased the amount of shrimp, in order to keep it moist). Mix all ingredients and dish over lettuce leaves and sprinkle with paprika.

CUT OFF

Clarisse Giambrone
LAFOURCHE PARISH

Creamy Pralines
MAKES 25

3/4 cup light brown sugar
3/4 cup sugar
1/2 cup evaporated milk
1/4 cup butter or oleo
1/4 tsp. cream of tartar
1 tsp. vanilla
1 cup pecan halves

Put two sheets of foil out first. Cook together sugars, milk and cream of tartar, stirring constantly until achieving firm soft ball stage or until thermometer reads 236 degrees. Remove from heat and add butter and vanilla. Stir until butter melts. Add pecans and beat until thick. Drop by small spoonfuls on foil.

DENHAM SPRINGS
Mannette France
LIVINGSTON PARISH

Fried Catfish
SERVES 4

2 lbs. catfish tenderloin
1 cup Season Fish Fry
1 cup Season Bread Crumbs
Cooking oil
Salt
Garlic salt
Season Salt
Hot sauce
Mustard

Heat oil. Season fish with salt, season salt, garlic salt, hot sauce and mustard. Mix Season Bread Crumbs and Fish Fry together. Bread each piece of fish. Drop one piece of fish at a time in hot oil. Cook until fish is golden brown.

DES ALLEMANDS
Elizabeth Warren
ST. CHARLES PARISH

Shrimp With Baby Lima Beans
SERVES 6

2 16 oz. cans baby lima beans, drained
2 cups peeled shrimp
3 cups water
1/2 cup flour
1/2 cup cooking oil
1/4 cup shallots, chopped
1/2 cup onions, chopped
1/2 cup bell pepper, chopped
1 tbsp. parsley
1/4 tsp. garlic, chopped
Salt and pepper to taste

Use thick pot. Heat oil and flour. Stir constantly until dark brown or caramel color roux is mixed (your choice). Turn heat very low and add shrimp to roux. Cook slowly until shrimp are pink color. Add all of the seasonings and lima beans. Saute' about 5 minutes. Add 3 cup of water. Simmer on low heat about 30 minutes or until thick. Add salt and pepper to taste. Serve over hot cooked rice.

DESTREHAN
Fay Walker Louque
ST. CHARLES PARISH

Crabmeat Au Gratin

SERVES 10

2 lbs. crabmeat
1 stick oleo
1 large onion, chopped
1/2 cup celery, chopped
10 oz. mild cheddar cheese, grated
2 egg yolks, slightly beaten
4 tbsp. flour
1 large and 1 small can Carnation evaporated milk
Bread crumbs
Salt and pepper to taste

Saute' onions and celery in oleo until soft. Blend flour and milk. Remove from heat. Add egg yolk, crabmeat, salt, pepper and cheese. Place in baking dish. Sprinkle top with bread crumbs. Bake for 20 minutes at 350 degrees. Very easy and very good!

DONALDSONVILLE

Brenda Giambrone
ASCENSION PARISH

Red Beans And Rice
SERVES 6

1 lb. red beans
3 quarts cold water
4 onions, chopped
4 toes garlic, chopped
2 lbs. smoked sausage
2 lb. ham trimmings with skin
Salt and pepper to taste

Pick over beans and wash thoroughly. Soak overnight. Boil beans with onion, ham and garlic over a strong heat using a heavy pot. When beans are tender add sausage that has been cut into 6 inch lengths. Continue to cook for 30 minutes adding more water as necessary. Adjust seasoning. Serve over steamed rice.

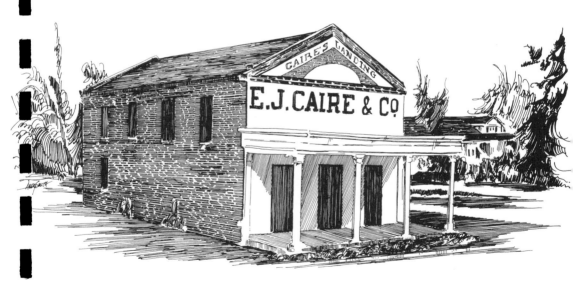

EDGARD

Virgie Marie Johnson
ST. JOHN THE BAPTIST PARISH

Jalapeno Corn Bread
SERVES 6-8

1 cup yellow corn meal
1 large onion, chopped
1 can cream corn
1 cup milk
1/2 lb. mild cheddar cheese, grated
1 lb. ground beef
1/2 cup cooking oil
2 eggs
3 chili peppers
1/2 tsp. baking soda
3/4 tbsp. salt

Combine corn meal, milk, eggs, cream corn, baking soda, salt and oil. Mix and set aside. Saute' beef and drain. Grease large skillet and heat. Sprinkle a very thin layer of corn meal in bottom of skillet and brown lightly. Pour in half of meal batter and sprinkle with grated cheese. Add a layer of meat. Top with chopped onions and chili peppers. Pour remaining batter on top. Bake 1 hour at 350 degrees or until golden brown. Sprinkle some cheese on top to brown. Bake in large black skillet.

ERWINVILLE

Pamela N. Lurry
WEST BATON ROUGE PARISH

Corn Casserole
SERVES 6

1 stick butter
1/2 cup water
1 cup (box) Jiffy Corn Bread Mix
2 eggs
2 cans cream style corn
1 small onion, chopped

Melt butter in 9" X 12" baking dish. Beat eggs and water. Add other ingredients and stir well. Pour over melted butter. Spread butter that will collect in corners over top of casserole. Bake at 350 degrees for 1 hour.

ETHEL
Beverly Shelby
EAST FELICIANA PARISH

Bread Pudding

SERVES 4-6

1 loaf stale French bread, cubed
2 quarts milk
2 cups sugar
1 tbsp. nutmeg
1 tbsp. vanilla
1/2 tbsp. cinnamon
6 eggs
1/2 box raisins
1/2 stick butter
1 apple, cored and sliced

Put French bread in large (4 quart) mixing bowl and add milk. Let soak about 5 minutes. Add remaining ingredients and mix well. Pour into a buttered 9" X 13" baking dish. Bake at 350 degrees for 1 hour or until toothpick inserted comes out clean. Cut into squares and serve.

FOLSOM
Earline L. Mauthe

ST. TAMMANY PARISH

Shrimp Delight

SERVES 6-8

1 stick margarine
2 1/2 cups shrimp, chopped
1 bunch shallots, chopped
1/4 cup parsley flakes
2 tbsp. flour
1 1/2-2 cups milk (may use cream)
1 tsp. Creole seasoning (Zatarains)
Red pepper
Salt
1 small jar mushrooms, drained
1/4 lb. Romano or Swiss cheese, grated

Melt margarine. Add shrimp and cook 2 minutes. Add shallots and parsley and saute'. Blend in flour and add milk. Stir until heated then add seasonings and mushrooms. Allow mixture to heat while gently stirring. Add cheese just before serving. Serve hot as an appetizer or dip or as an entree over rice, pasta or potatoes. (I like to use leftover turkey or chicken in place of the shrimp.)

FRANKLINTON

Darlene H. Jones
WASHINGTON PARISH

Sauce Patate (Potato Stew)
SERVES 6

1 cup all purpose flour
2/3 cup cooking oil
3 lbs. Irish potatoes, diced
1 lb. sausage or andouille
3 medium onions, chopped
1 small bell pepper, chopped
3 1/2 cups of water
1 tbsp. garlic, minced
2 stalks celery, chopped
Red pepper and salt to taste

Make roux with flour and oil and cook until dark. Then add onions, garlic, bell pepper and celery. Stirring often, cook until onions become watery. Then add 3 1/2 cups water, sausage, diced potatoes, salt and red pepper. Cover and cook on low heat stirring occasionally. Dish is done when potatoes are cooked and start to crumble. Serve over rice.

FRENCH SETTLEMENT
Atrice Gore
LIVINGSTON PARISH

Phyllis' Yummy Pork N' Beans
SERVES 8-12

1/2 lb. bacon
1 large onion, diced
1 small bell pepper, diced
2 large cans Pork n' Beans
3/4 cup light brown sugar

Brown bacon until crispy, drain fat. Add onion and bell pepper and saute' on medium heat. Add beans and sugar and cook for 1/2 hour on low heat. Eat and enjoy.

GALLIANO
Phyllis Champagne
LAFOURCHE PARISH

"Vita Monica's Spaghetti Gravy"
SERVES 8-10

2 12 oz. cans tomato paste OR
1 can tomato paste and 1 can tomato sauce
1 medium onion, chopped
1 small garlic, chopped (8-10 cloves)
1 tbsp. green pepper, chopped
1 tsp. dry basil leaves
1 cauliflower
10 to 12 cups water
2/3 cup sugar
1 or 2 fennels, chopped
Salt and pepper to taste

Saute' onion, garlic and green pepper in 1/4 cup of oil. Add tomato paste or one can of tomato paste and one can of tomato sauce if desired. Add 10 to 12 cups of water, basil, sugar, salt and pepper. Break flowerettes off of cauliflower and fry in a little oil. Put cauliflower in gravy and cook for 3 hours. Boil spaghetti (in water with 1/4 cup oil and 1 or 2 chopped fennels added) until done. Serve gravy over spaghetti.

GARYVILLE
Mrs. Sidney J. Levet III
ST. JOHN THE BAPTIST PARISH

Eggplant Dressing
SERVES 12-16

4 eggplants, diced
2 medium onions, chopped
1 bunch green onions, chopped
1 lb. package whole hog sausage
4 cloves garlic, chopped
1 stick butter

2 ribs celery, chopped
1/2 green pepper, chopped
1/2 cup Parmesan cheese
Seasoned bread crumbs
Salt
Black pepper
Red pepper

Peel and dice eggplant into 2 inch squares. Boil in salt water until tender and drain. Cook sausage and crumble, then drain off grease. After you take out sausage and drain grease, put in the same skillet 1 stick of butter, onions, garlic, celery and green pepper. Cook down. When all vegetables are tender add sausage back into this mixture and heat well for 5 to 10 minutes. Add drained eggplant and seasoned bread crumbs and Parmesan cheese. Season with salt and red and black peppers. Mix well and put in casserole. Heat 20 minutes in 350 degree oven or heat in microwave until hot and bubbly.

GEISMAR
Olivia Young
ASCENSION PARISH

Crayfish Fettucine
SERVES 8

1 1/2 blocks margarine
3 pieces of green onion, chopped
2 pieces of celery, chopped
2 large onions, chopped
1 large bell pepper, chopped
1 1/2 lbs. crayfish
3 pieces of garlic, chopped
1 small can Pet milk or
1 pint Half N' Half milk
1/2 can jalapeno relish

1/2 lb. Velveeta cheese
1/2 lb. flat noodles or fettucine noodles
1 tsp. flour
1 tsp. parsley
Black pepper
Salt
1 tsp. liquid crab boil

Marinate crayfish with 1 tsp. of liquid crab boil for about 1 hour. Saute' onions, bell pepper, celery and green onions in margarine until soft. Add flour, parsley, crayfish and let cook about 15 minutes. Add jalapeno relish, Velveeta cheese, Half N' Half milk and garlic. Let cook 15 minutes. Cook fettucine noodles until tender, drain, mix with crayfish mixture. Put in casserole dish, sprinkle with Parmesan cheese and bake at 350 degrees for about 15 minutes. (Note: Instead of crayfish, you may use shrimp or shrimp and crabmeat. Some people also use chicken.)

GIBSON

Ruth Sanchez
TERREBONNE PARISH

Shrimp Potato Stew
SERVES 6

1/4 cup cooking oil
1 onion, chopped
1 lb small raw shrimp, peeled
8 medium potatoes, peeled and cubed
1 tbsp. parsley, finely chopped
6 cups boiling water
Salt and pepper to taste

In a 4 quart sauce pan, heat oil on medium setting. Add onions and cook until brown. Add shrimp and simmer for 10 minutes. Stir in cubed potatoes, parsley, boiling water and salt and pepper. Cook for 60 minutes. Serve over rice. (Meat products such as corned beef, cubed round steak or Vienna Sausage may be substituted for shrimp).

GOLDEN MEADOW
Cindy Lefort
LAFOURCHE PARISH

Chicken Jambalaya
SERVES 6-8

1 5 to 6 lb. hen, cut into serving pieces
3 cups long grain rice, uncooked
1 cup cooking oil
3 cups onions, chopped fine
3 tsp. salt
2 tsp. granulated garlic
1/2 cup green onions, chopped
1/4 cup bell peppers, chopped
1/2 tsp. black pepper
2 1/2 tsp. Louisiana hot sauce

Fry chicken in cooking oil until dark brown. Remove cooking oil leaving just enough cooking oil to cover the bottom of pot. Add onions and cook with chicken until onions are dark brown. Add about 1/2 cup of water and then put in bell peppers and green onions. Let simmer for about 10 minutes. Add about 5 cups of water and remaining seasoning. Then bring water to a rolling boil. Add rice and stir. Let rice and water boil until water thickens and turn rice over once. Do not stir as this will break the rice up. Cover with tight fitting lid and let simmer on a low fire for about 10 minutes. Turn one more time and let set for about 10 more minutes and then your jambalaya is ready to eat.

GONZALES
Charles Breaux/Ricky Breaux
ASCENSION PARISH

Cabbage And Andouille Gumbo
SERVES 6

1/2 cup flour
1/2 cup oil
1 large onion, chopped
1/2 cup sweet pepper, chopped
3/4 cup shallots, chopped
3 cloves garlic, chopped
1 small head cabbage, chopped fine
1 large andouille, skinned and sliced
2 1/2 quarts of water
File' to taste
Salt and pepper to taste

Make roux with flour and oil. Add onion, sweet pepper, shallots, garlic and saute' for 10 minutes. Add andouille and saute' again for 20 minutes, covered. Add water and cook for 1/2 hour. Add chopped cabbage and cook for 25 minutes. Let set for 1 hour before serving. Serve over hot rice. Add file' and enjoy.

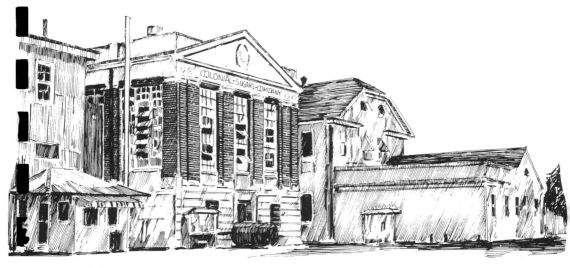

GRAMERCY

Lillian Simon
ST. JAMES PARISH

Chicken Pillard
SERVES 8

1 chicken, cut in bite size pieces
3/4 stick oleo
1 can cream of chicken soup
1 can French onion soup
1 cup chicken broth
1 1/2 cups raw rice
1 package of 4 chicken breast halves
1 small bell pepper, chopped
1 4 oz. jar pimento
1 tsp. lemon pepper
1 tsp. salt
1 tbsp. parsley flakes
Dash of Tabasco

Boil chicken, debone and save broth. Place chicken in dish.
Melt oleo. Combine with all soups and raw rice and add all
seasonings. Add all to chicken. Bake in covered casserole
for 1 hour and 15 minutes at 350 degrees. Uncover and bake
an additional 15 minutes.

GREENSBURG

Toffie Ainsworth Smith
ST. HELENA PARISH

Mama's Chicken
SERVES 5

1 whole chicken or
12 pieces of chicken
1 10 3/4 oz. cream of mushroom soup
1 medium onion, chopped
Creole seasoning
Garlic powder

Season chicken with Creole seasoning and garlic powder.
Place chicken in skillet and cook for 5 minutes. Add onions.
Cook until clear. Empty can of cream of mushroom soup into
skillet. Add 1/2 can water. Stir. Cook until chicken is completely cooked. Stir occasionally. Serve over rice.

GRETNA

Helen Thigpen
JEFFERSON PARISH

Best Crabmeat Casserole

SERVES 6

1/4 cup butter
1 onion, chopped
2 tbsp. flour
1 1/4 cup milk
5 oz. cheddar cheese, grated
1 lb. crabmeat
French bread or crackers
Cayenne pepper
Pepper
Salt

Saute' onion in butter. When soft, add flour and stir until bubbly. Add milk, cook and stir until thick. Remove from heat. Add 1/2 of the cheese and all crabmeat. Season to taste. Pour in casserole and top with remaining cheese. Bake at 350 degrees for approximately 30 minutes or until bubbly and cheese melts. Serve with Ritz crackers or on French bread. Can be prepared in microwave and turns out equally well. Adjust cooking time depending on your oven.

HAHNVILLE

Laurie S. Goodell
ST. CHARLES PARISH

48

Seafood Casserole

SERVES 10

1 lb. crabmeat
1/2 lb. crawfish tails
1 lb. shrimp
2 onions, chopped
1 small bell pepper, chopped
3/4 cup celery, chopped
1 can sliced mushrooms
1 stick butter
1/2 cup flour
1 can evaporated milk
1 can water
1 tsp. sugar
1/2 lb. American or Swiss cheese, grated
Bread crumbs
Salt and pepper to taste

Make a white sauce of butter, flour and milk. Saute' celery, onions, bell pepper and mushrooms. Add white crabmeat, crawfsh and boiled shrimp to sauted onion mixture. Cook 10 minutes. Add to white sauce. Mix well. If too thick, add more milk. Put mixture in buttered casserole dish and top with bread crumbs and cheese. Bake at 350 degrees for 25 minutes. This may also be used for seafood crepes.

HAMMOND

Nita Lunn
TANGIPAHOAPARISH

Wild Rice Casserole

SERVES 12

1 cup wild rice
1 package Uncle Ben's Brown Wild Rice
1 onion, chopped
Mushrooms, sliced
6 round Italian sausage
2 cans cream of mushroom soup
Butter
Red pepper to taste

Cook Uncle Ben's Rice according to directions. Prepare wild rice according to directions. Brown sausage, drain and crumble. Saute' onions and mushrooms in butter. Combine both rices, sausage, onions, mushrooms and add cream of mushroom soup and red pepper. Bake uncovered in 350 degree oven for about 45 minutes.

HARVEY

Cindy Dike
JEFFERSON PARISH

Mommee's Stuffed Bell Peppers
SERVES 12

12 medium bell peppers
2 1/2 lbs. ground meat
5 medium yellow onions, chopped
1 cup cooked rice
Salt and pepper to taste
Italian bread crumbs

Cut the tops off of the bell peppers. Cut only about 1/2 inch from top. (Do not cut in half as the peppers have a tendency to flop open.) Save tops. Clean bell peppers. Boil the cut and cleaned bell peppers for about 4 minutes being sure not to over boil. Chop the tops of the uncooked bell peppers and onions while browning ground meat. Drain meat and add chopped peppers and onions. Cook over low flame until soft, season to taste and add rice. Stuff peppers with meat mixture. Sprinkle tops with Italian bread crumbs. Place on cookie sheet and bake for 20 minutes at 350 degrees or until bread crumbs begin to brown.

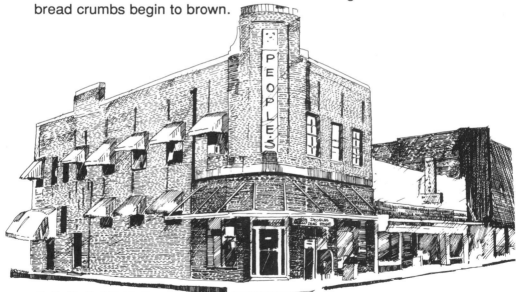

HOUMA
Odette Blanchard Chamberlain
TERREBONNE PARISH

Touch Of Italy Casserole
SERVES 6-8

2 cans artichoke hearts
2 cans French style green beans
1/2 cup Italian bread crumbs
1/2 cup Parmesan cheese
Juice of 1 lemon
3 to 4 cloves garlic, chopped
Olive oil

Pour artichoke hearts in pot with liquid, bring to boil and pour off liquid. Cut in halves. Drain liquid off green beans and mix with artichoke hearts. Add bread crumbs, cheese, garlic and lemon juice. Mix well and place in casserole dish. Pour olive oil over top. Bake 30 minutes at 350 degrees.

INDEPENDENCE

Virginia G. Patanella
TANGIPAHOA PARISH

Chicken And Dumplings
SERVES 6-8

Chicken
2 cups self rising flour
1 1/2 cups milk
Salt and pepper to taste

Disjoint chicken (can use a large fryer or a hen, hen has a stronger flavor and more fat). Simmer chicken until tender in enough water to keep covered. Add salt and pepper to taste (approximately 1 1/2 tsp. salt and 1/4 tsp. pepper). Remove chicken from broth (can remove meat from bone if you desire). Combine flour and enough milk to make a stiff dough. Shape mixture into a ball and roll to a thickness of 1/8 inch on a lightly floured board. Cut into 1 to 1 1/2 inch strips. Drop into rapidly boiling broth; if there is not enough broth add hot water. Cover, reduce heat and simmer 8 to 10 minutes. Remove cover and add 1 cup whole milk and bring back to a simmer. Add chicken and remove from heat. NOTE: For a more tender Dumpling you may cut 1/3 cup shortening into flour.

JACKSON

Melba A. Wesley
EAST FELICIANA PARISH

Vegetable Casserole
SERVES 10

1 can Veg-All, slightly drained
1 cup onion, chopped
3/4 cup mayonnaise
1/2 stick margarine
1 cup yellow cheese, grated
1 8 oz. can water chestnuts, sliced
1 1/2 cup Ritz crackers, crushed

Cook onion in margarine. Combine mayonnaise, Veg-All, cheese and sliced water chestnuts. Add onion to margarine mixture. Place in casserole and cover with cracker crumbs. Bake at 350 degrees until bubbly and brown (about 40 minutes).

KENTWOOD
Willie Merle White
TANGIPAHOA PARISH

Shrimp Fettucine
SERVES 4

1/2 cup butter
1 lb. shrimp, peeled
2 cloves garlic, chopped
1 onion, chopped
6 oz. fettucine noodles,
cooked and drained
2 tbsp. butter
1/2 cup Parmesan cheese
Salt and red pepper to taste

Melt 1/2 cup butter in a saucepan. Stir in shrimp, onion,
garlic, salt and red pepper. Saute' until onions are wilted.
Toss fettucine noodles with 2 tbsp. butter and Parmesan
cheese until coated. Serve over warm fettucine.

LAPLACE
Brenda Madere
ST. JOHN THE BAPTIST PARISH

Baked Brisket
SERVES 15-20

1 brisket
2 cups Jack Miller Barbecue Sauce
1/2 cup Worcestershire sauce
2 cups water
Charcoal for pit
Cajun seasoning

Trim fat from brisket. Rub Cajun seasoning and
Worcestershire sauce over entire brisket. Place in shallow
baking pan and pour barbecue sauce and water over brisket.
Refrigerate overnight. Light barbecue pit. Get coals very hot.
Brown brisket well on both sides. Remove from pit and place
in oven and bake at 200 degrees for 10 hours or until very
tender. Remove from oven. Slice very thin with electric knife.
Ideal for parties!

LABADIEVILLE
Rita Falgoust
ASSUMPTION PARISH

Venison Roast

SERVES 10

4 to 6 lb. venison roast
4 strips bacon
Italian salad dressing
1 tbsp. cooking oil
1 cup water
2 cloves garlic
1/2 cup onions, chopped
Red and black pepper
Salt

With sharp knife make deep holes across grain of meat. Mix garlic, onions, salt and peppers and insert into holes topping with pieces of bacon. Marinate overnight in Italian dressing. Cook meat in a heavy pot with water and oil. When it comes to a boil, put lid on pot and cook on low heat for 4 to 6 hours. If gravy is desired, thicken with cornstarch.

LIVINGSTON
Iris Stilley
LIVINGSTON PARISH

Crawfish Fettucine
SERVES 16

1 stick margarine
2 medium onions, chopped
1 bell pepper, chopped
2 cloves garlic, chopped
1/4 cup plain flour
3 lbs. crawfish tails
1 cup milk
1 lb. Velveeta cheese
1/4 lb. Velveeta jalapeno cheese
1 lb. fine fettucine noodles, cooked
Green onions
Black and red pepper
Salt

Melt margarine in large saucepan. Saute' onions, bell peppers, garlic and cook until tender (about 15 minutes). Add flour, stir and cook 15 minutes. Stir frequently as mixture may stick. Add green onion and crawfish tails. Cook covered for 15 minutes, stir occasionally. Add milk, cheese and salt and pepper to taste. Cook covered on low heat for 30 minutes. Cook fettucine according to package. Mix crawfish mixture and noodles thoroughly. Pour into greased casserole. Sprinkle top with shredded cheese. Bake 350 degrees for 15 to 20 minutes. NOTE: Shrimp may be substituted for crawfish.

LIVONIA
Donna LeJeune
POINTE COUPEE PARISH

Apricot Cheese Delight Salad
SERVES 12

FILLING:
1 17 oz. can apricots, drained
and chopped fine
1 large can crushed
pineapple, drained
2 packages orange gelatin
2 cups hot water
1 cup apricot juice
1 cup miniature marshmallows
3/4 cup cheddar cheese, grated

TOPPING:
1/2 cup sugar
3 tbsp. flour
1 egg, slightly beaten
2 tbsp. butter
1 cup pineapple juice
1 cup whipping cream,
whipped

Keep apricot and pineapple juice separate. Chill fruit.
Dissolve gelatin in hot water. Add apricot juice (save
pineapple juice for topping) and fold in apricots, pineapple and
marshmallows. Chill until firm then add topping. TOPPING:
Combine sugar and flour and blend in egg and butter. Add
pineapple juice and cook over low heat, stirring constantly
until thickened. Let cool. Fold in whipping cream and spread
over congealed salad. Sprinkle with grated cheese and chill
thoroughly. Cut in squares and serve in lettuce.

LOCKPORT
Joyce Souther
LAFOURCHE PARISH

Corn Soup
SERVES 8-10

10 ears of corn
1 lb. pickle meat
1 can tomato sauce
1/2 cup ketchup
6 potatoes, cut in pieces
1 cup green lima beans, optional
1 onion, chopped
1/2 bell pepper, chopped
2 tbsp. cooking oil
3 quarts water
Salt and pepper to taste

Cut corn off cob, scraping with knife. Smother corn, meat, onion and bell pepper in cooking oil for 30 minutes. Add tomato sauce and ketchup and cook for 15 minutes. Add 2 quarts of water and let boil for 30 minutes. Add lima beans and cut potatoes. Salt and pepper to taste and add 1 quart of water. Let boil until potatoes are done. If too thick add 2 cups water and bring to a boil.

LULING
Florence Pitre
ST. CHARLES PARISH

Jambalaya

SERVES 12

4 lbs. fresh sausage
4 onions, chopped
4 sticks celery, chopped
1 green pepper, chopped
1 large can tomatoes
3 cans beef broth
4 cups raw rice
1/4 cup green onions,
chopped (shallots)
Salt and pepper to taste

Fry sausage, then take out and cook down onions, celery and green pepper. Add large can tomatoes. Cook a few minutes. Add water to beef broth to make 6 cups. Bring to a boil and simmer for 30 minutes. While simmering, add sausage (cut into bite size pieces), salt and pepper. Add 4 cups raw rice. Bring to a boil for 3 minutes. Turn heat on low and cover pot. After 15 minutes of cooking, remove cover and stir with fork. Cover again and keep hot on low fire for 15 to 20 minutes. Add chopped green onions during last 5 minutes of cooking.

LUTCHER

Yvette L. Dornier
ST. JAMES PARISH

Bettie's Dirty Rice
SERVES 8

1 1/2 cup uncooked rice
1 large onion, chopped
1 bell pepper, chopped
1 can cream of mushroom soup
1 soup can of water
1 1/2 cup uncooked ground beef
1 can French onion soup
1 can cream of chicken soup
Salt, pepper and garlic powder to taste

Mix all together. Put in a large greased baking dish. Cover with foil. Bake 1 1/2 hours at 325 degrees. Stir occasionally.

MADISONVILLE

Bettie Davenport
ST TAMMANY PARISH

Crab Cakes
SERVES 5

1 lb. white crabmeat
1 tbsp. tub margarine
1/4 cup sweet pepper, minced
1/4 cup parsley, minced
1/2 cup green onion, minced
1/2 tsp. salt
1/4 tsp. cayenne pepper
1 egg white
1 tbsp. mayonnaise
1 tsp. Worcestershire sauce
1 tsp. prepared mustard
3/4 cup bread crumbs

In a skillet with margarine saute' sweet pepper, parsley and green onion for 5 minutes. Add crabmeat, salt and cayenne pepper. Cook for 3 minutes. Remove from heat and cool. Mix egg white, mayonnaise, worcestershire sauce and mustard all together. Mix this and bread crumbs with crab mixture. Form into 10 patties, coat with bread crumbs and dot with margarine. Bake in 400 degree oven for 30 minutes to get good crisp patties. Bake in a heavy iron skillet. This is a good low cholesterol recipe.

MANDEVILLE
Betty Pellegrin
ST. TAMMANY PARISH

The Best Pinto Beans Ever

SERVES 8

1 lb. Camellia Pinto Beans
12 cups of water
1 onion, chopped
1 clove garlic
3 strips crisp fried bacon
4 drops McIhenny Tabasco Sauce
Salt and pepper to taste

Rinse and sort beans. Cover with water and boil gently for 15 minutes. Then start over with fresh water and let come to a boil. Saute' onion and garlic until wilted and add to beans. Cook for 1 hour and 45 minutes on medium heat. Add salt, pepper, Tabasco and crispy fried bacon and cook for 15 minutes or until done.

MARINGOUIN

Bessie Cashio
IBERVILLE PARISH

No Worry Jambalaya
SERVES 4-6

1 stick oleo
1 onion, chopped
1 bell pepper, chopped
1 stalk celery, chopped
1 1/2 cup rice
1 large can broth
1 3 oz. can mushrooms with liquid
1 can Trappey's black eye peas
10 inches of sausage
2 deboned chicken breast, cut in narrow strips
Creole seasoning to taste

In automatic rice cooker, melt margarine. In separate frying pan, brown sausage which has been sliced and chicken breasts strips. Add onion, bell pepper, celery, rice, broth, mushrooms and peas to the rice cooker. Stir well. Add sausage and chicken and Creole seasonings to the rice cooker. Put the lid on the cooker and cook for 45 minutes (20 minutes on cook and 25 minutes on warm). NOTE: shrimp may be substituted for the chicken and sausage, but it should be cooked slightly before adding to cooker.

MAUREPAS
Gerald Bantaa
LIVINGSTON PARISH

Artichoke And Snap Bean Casserole
SERVES 10

2 large cans French style green beans, liquid included
2 cups Progresso seasoned bread crumbs
2 large cans artichoke hearts, chopped
1/2 cup olive oil
2 cups Romano or Italian cheese
4 medium onions, chopped
6 cloves garlic, chopped

Simmer onions and garlic in olive oil. Add snap beans and liquid. Stir. Add bread crumbs, artichoke hearts and cheese. Mix well. Put in casserole dish and bake at 350 degrees for about 20 minutes or until well heated. NOTE: Very little salt is needed.

METAIRIE
Phyllis H. Romano
JEFFERSON PARISH

Cajun Spicy Steak
SERVES 6

2 lbs. number 7 steak
1 10 oz. can Rotel tomatoes
1 tbsp. oil
1 16 oz. can whole tomatoes
1 onion, sliced
1 green pepper, sliced
2 tbsp. flour
1 tsp. salt
1/4 tsp. pepper

Trim fat from meat. Cut steak into thin strips. Combine flour, salt and pepper. Coat meat with seasoned flour. In large pan, brown meat on both sides in hot oil. Add onions and green pepper. Continue cooking 5 minutes. Then add Rotel and whole tomatoes. Cover and simmer 1 to 1 1/2 hours until tender. Serve over rice. NOTE: 270 calories each serving.

MONTEGUT

Wendy N. Bergeron
TERREBONNE PARISH

CO-DE-OS (French Donuts)

SERVES 4-5

2 cups flour
2 1/2 tbsp. sugar
2 tbsp. baking powder
1 tsp. salt
1 egg
1/2 cup warm water

Mix ingredients together to a sticky consistency, adding a little water if necessary. Turn out on floured surface and roll to 1/2 inch thickness and cut into small squares (a pizza cutter works great). Pull each square thin and drop in hot grease and fry until golden brown. May be served with butter, syrup or powdered sugar. "My French-Acadian grandmother always cooked these for us for Sunday breakfast."

MORGANZA

Diane R. Grantham
POINTE COUPEE PARISH

Chicken Bake Dinner
SERVES 4

4 quarter pieces chicken OR
4 chicken breasts
1 large onion, sliced
1/4 cup bell pepper, chopped
1 can mushrooms OR
1 large handful sliced fresh mushrooms
4 large potatoes cut in half
1 cup water
Salt
Pepper
Seasonall

Place everything in baking dish. Bake in moderate oven at 350 degrees for 1 to 1 1/2 hours depending on size of chicken pieces. Serve chicken and potatoes side by side on plate. The rest of the ingredients may be spooned over a serving of hot rice. More water should be added during cooking as this will form a natural gravy.

NAPOLEONVILLE
Judy Landry
ASSUMPTION PARISH

Stuffed Mirlitons (Vegetable Pears)
SERVES 6

6 to 8 medium mirlitons
1 medium onion, chopped
2 pods garlic, minced
1 lb. medium shrimp, cleaned, deveined, cut in half
1/2 box Stove Top Stuffing
1 tbsp. oil
1/4 cup bread crumbs
Salt and pepper to taste

Boil mirlitons until fork tender, approximately 45 minutes. Cut in half. Let cool. Remove and discard seed. Scoop out pulp while leaving shell intact. Put pulp in colander to drain. Saute' onions and garlic in oil until clear. Add pulp and saute' uncovered on medium heat 30 minutes or until most liquid is absorbed. Stir occasionally. Add shrimp and cook 10 minutes. Mix prepared stuffing according to directions for dry stuffing and add. Mix well. Fill shells with mixture. Sprinkle with bread crumbs and put a dab of butter on each. Bake at 350 degrees for approximately 30 minutes.
NOTE: Optional-Add 1/4 cup of white wine to mixture before filling shells.

NEW ORLEANS
Wilhelmina Maheu
ORLEANS PARISH

Parlange Seafood Casserole
SERVES 12

4 lbs. shrimp, cooked and peeled
1 1/2 lbs. crabmeat
6 cups brown rice, cooked
3 1/2 cups onions, chopped
4 cloves of garlic
2 bell peppers, chopped
6 tsp. Worcestershire sauce
Tabasco, several dashes
Tony Chachere's, several big dashes
Creole seasoning or Spike seasoning
Olive oil

Mix ingredients together. Pour a little olive oil over all. Cook in 350 degree oven in casserole dish covered with foil. Bake for 35 or 40 minutes. Remove foil for last 5 minutes of cooking.

PARLANGE PLANTATION, NEW ROADS, LA.

NEW ROADS
Lucy Brandon Parlange
POINTE COUPEE PARISH

Crab Spaghetti

SERVES 15-20

1 lb. loose crabmeat
5 12oz. cans of Hunt's tomato paste
1 1/2 dozen cleaned crabs
4 tbsp. crab boil or to taste
3 bell peppers, chopped
1 stalk celery, chopped
3 onions, chopped
1 head garlic, chopped
1 lb. spaghetti
Salt and pepper

In a 12 quart pot, saute' all seasoning in a little cooking oil until tender. Add tomato paste, crabmeat and cleaned crabs. Fill pot 3/4 full of water until tomato paste is dissolved. Add crab boil and salt until desired taste is achieved. Lower heat and let cook about 3 hours. Do not add pepper until almost cooked. Meanwhile cook 1 lb. of spaghetti as directed on package. Serve sauce over spaghetti. This dish freezes wonderfully.

NORCO

Melanie G. Duvic
ST. CHARLES PARISH

Ro-tel Chicken
SERVES 8

6 chicken breasts
1 lb. Velveeta
1 12 oz. package vermicelli
1 small jar sliced mushrooms
1 small jar diced pimentos
1 can LeSeur peas, drained
1 can diced Rotel tomatoes (in juice)
Salt and pepper to taste

Boil and debone chicken, reserving approximately 3 cups of broth. Prepare vermicelli as directed and drain. Add to vermicelli, chicken and remaining ingredients (drained peas only) and reserved chicken broth. Cook on low heat until cheese is melted and liquid is absorbed. May add salt and pepper to taste.

NORWOOD
Ellyn Toney Boatner
EAST FELICIANA PARISH

Crawfish Pie

MAKES 18-24

INGREDIENTS

1 lb. crawfish tails
1 stick of margarine
1/4 cup green onions, chopped
1 cup white onions, chopped
1 can cream of mushroom soup
1 small can of evaporated milk
1 tbsp. cornstarch
Red pepper and salt to taste
18 to 24 small Bama pie shells

Preheat oven to 350 degrees. Saute' the white onions in margarine. Add can of cream of mushroom soup. Blend the cornstarch in the evaporated milk first, then add to the mixture. Saute' until everything is well blended. Add green onions, crawfish and seasoning (salt and pepper or Tony's seasoning, "I use Tony's"). Continue to saute' for approximately 10 more minutes. Total cooking time will be approximately 20 minutes. Fill pie shell with mixture. (If making large pie, cover with other pie shell and slit the top). Place in a preheated 350 degree oven and bake for 30 minutes or until golden brown. One pound will make approximately 18 to 24 small pies. "I use Bama frozen pie shells which come 8 to a box."

PAINCOURTVILLE

Joy R. Banta
ASSUMPTION PARISH

Alligator Sauce Piquante
SERVES 6

2 lbs. alligator
1/4 cup oil or margarine
1 1/2 cups B. B. Q. sauce
1 can tomato paste, small
2 cans tomato sauce, small
1 1/2 cups rice, cooked
2 lemons, halved

2 cups water
2 cloves garlic
1 medium onion, chopped
3 shallots, chopped
1 small bell pepper, chopped
Parsley
Salt and pepper to taste

Boil alligator and 2 lemons "halved" for 1 to 1 1/2 hours. Drain and set aside. In a 5 quart saucepan, add oil or margarine, garlic, onion, shallots, bell pepper and parsley. Saute' for 2 minutes, then stir in 1 to 1 1/2 cups B. B. Q. sauce, tomato paste, tomato sauce and water. Stir. Add alligator. Cook on medium to low heat for 1 hour or to taste. Serve over cooked rice.

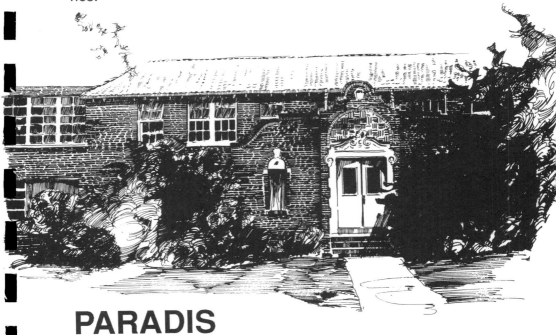

PARADIS
Pamela Rogers
ST. CHARLES PARISH

Crawfish Patties
SERVES 9

5 large onions
3 cloves garlic
4 sticks celery
1 big bell pepper
3 eggs
1/2 cup bread crumbs
Fish fry or flour
6 lbs. ground crawfish tails
Salt and pepper to taste

Grind crawfish tails with all seasonings. Add 3 eggs and salt
and pepper to taste. Add bread crumbs. Mix together well.
Form into patties, then coat with fish fry or flour. Deep fry
until brown.

PIERRE PART
Mrs. Marie Gaudet
ASSUMPTION PARISH

Fried Venison
SERVES SEVERAL

Venison tenderloin, sliced thin
Tony Chachere's Fry All
Louisiana Hot Sauce

Marinate in Louisiana Hot Sauce all day (coat meat well, maybe using the whole bottle, depending on how much meat you have). Coat meat with Tony Chachere's Fry All. Deep fry 2 or 3 minutes or until golden brown.

PLAINS
Lynn Waddell
EAST BATON ROUGE PARISH

Corn Bread Dressing

SERVES 12

3 cups celery, chopped
2 cups shallots, chopped
2 pones corn bread
3 cans chicken broth (No Water)
3 cans cream of chicken soup
1 sleeve crackers

9 eggs, slightly beaten
6 pieces white bread
1/2 tsp. salt
1 tsp. onion salt
1 tsp. garlic powder
1 tsp. black pepper

Crumble breads together and mix all ingredients together. Add water to make soupy. Bake at 350 degrees for about 11/2 to 2 hours. (Chicken pieces may be added.)

PLAQUEMINE

Cheryl D. Hargooa
IBERVILLE PARISH

Raye's Cajun Fettucine
SERVES 8

1 1/2 cup butter
2 medium yellow onions, chopped
2 medium bell peppers, chopped
2 cloves garlic,chopped
Salt
1/2 bunch fresh parsley
1 pint Half N' Half
1 oz. lemon juice
1 8 oz. regular Velveeta,
   shredded
1 8 oz. Mexican Velveeta,
   shredded
3 lbs. crawfish or shrimp
1 lb. crabmeat
1 lb. fettucine noodles
1/4 cup flour

Cook noodles according to package directions. In a 12 quart roaster, melt butter and saute' onions, peppers and garlic for about 15 minutes. Add salt to taste. Stir in flour slowly. Continue to stir steadily while it cooks for 10 minutes. Add parsley and allow to soften in mixture. Keep stirring. Add Half N' Half, lemon juice and cheese. Continue to stir until well blended. Add shrimp or crawfish and crabmeat. Cook about 20 minutes. Add noodles and serve.

POINT A LA HACHE

Raye Vodopic'
PLAQUEMINES PARISH

Strawberry Torte

SERVES 6-8

4 egg whites
1 cup sugar
1 cup pecans, chopped
1/2 cup saltine cracker crumbs
1 tsp. vanilla
1 tsp. baking powder
Dash of salt
Large container of Cool Whip
2 cans strawberry pie mix (Lucky Leaf brand)

Beat egg whites with salt and vanilla until foamy. Add sugar gradually. Beat until stiff peaks are formed. Mix nuts, crumbs and baking powder and fold into egg white mixture. Spread in well greased 9" X 13" pan. Bake in slow oven at 300 degrees for 40 minutes or until lightly brown. Cool completely. When cooled, add 1/2 Cool Whip and strawberry pie filling. Top with remaining Cool Whip. Refrigerate several hours before serving.

PONCHATOULA

Mrs. Hazel R. Dickerson
TANGIPAHOA PARISH

Crab Shrimp Casserole
SERVES 6-8

1 lb. left over boiled shrimp
2 cans crab meat
1/2 cup onions, chopped
1/2 cup celery, chopped
1/4 cup bell pepper, chopped
1/4 cup pimento, chopped
2 cups cooked rice
1 tsp. red pepper
1/2 tsp. salt
1 cup mayonnaise
1 cup evaporated milk
1 tsp. Lea and Perrin

Saute' onions, celery and peppers in butter. Mix all and bake
in uncovered dish at 375 degrees for 1 hour.

PORT ALLEN
Fern Dupuy
WEST BATON ROUGE PARISH

Chicken Bon Fon
SERVES 4

1 package chicken legs
1 package chicken thighs
2 lbs. bacon, cubed
3 large onions, cut-up
5 large potatoes, cubed
1 can beef consomme'
Salt
Pepper

Put cubed bacon, cut-up onions and chicken in electric skillet and simmer for 2 hours. Spoon out grease as needed. Cube potatoes and lightly fry. Add potatoes and consomme'. Let all ingredients simmer for 1 hour.

PORT SULPHUR
Robert Domingue
PLAQUEMINES PARISH

Stuffed Baked Rabbit
SERVES 8-10

3 rabbits, back legs and back
1 large onion, chopped
2 bunches green onions, chopped
6 large garlic cloves, chopped
Black pepper
Tony Chachere's Seasoning

Leave rabbits whole, they are easier to stuff when left
whole. Cut up onions, green onions and garlic and mix
together with Tony's and black pepper. Set aside 1/2 cup of
this mixture as it will be used later. Cut deep slits in
both sides of bones in legs and back. Stuff the above
seasoned mixture in holes. Place in deep pan and cover with
foil. Put in 350 degree oven for 2 hours. Remove foil and
brown on both sides. When real tender add 2 cups water and
the rest of seasoning mixture (1/2 cup) that was set aside to
make the gravy. Bake 30 more minutes. Serve over rice with
homemade biscuits.

PORT VINCENT
Nancy Smiley
LIVINGSTON PARISH

Shrimp Okra Creole Gumbo
SERVES 8-10

3 large onions, chopped
3/4 tsp. garlic powder
3/4 cup green onion, chopped
Fresh parsley
1 1/2 cups fresh smothered okra
3 lbs. fresh shrimp
1 cup flour
1 cup oil
Salt, black and red pepper to taste

In a iron pot add flour and oil and cook until a dark brown roux is achieved. Add onions to roux and simmer for a few minutes until they become clear. Add shrimp and stir until they become pink, about 5 minutes. After shrimp is pink add okra and 2 quarts water. Cook for 1 hour and add green onions, parsley, salt, pepper and red pepper. Also add 1/2 quart water and let cook for about 20 minutes more. Gumbo file' can be added if desired.

PRAIRIEVILLE
Mary Jane Brown
ASCENSION PARISH

Turtle Sauce Piquante
SERVES 12

4 or 5 lbs. turtle meat	1 8 oz. can tomato paste
2 cups onions, chopped	7 cups water
2 cups celery, chopped	1 4 oz. can mushrooms
1 cup bell pepper chopped	1 tsp. sugar
1 cup cooking oil	4 garlic pods, chopped fine
1 large can tomato juice	Salt, Tabasco sauce and
1 large can whole tomatoes	black pepper
2 8 oz. cans tomato sauce	1/2 cup onion tops and
	parsley, chopped

Cook meat (chicken, rabbit or shrimp can be substituted) over a low fire until tender or done. Remove meat and set aside. Add onions, celery and bell pepper to oil. Cook slowly until wilted. Add tomato juice, whole tomatoes, tomato paste, tomato sauce and 5 cups water. Cook over a medium fire until oil floats above tomatoes. Add meat, mushrooms, sugar and garlic. Season to taste with salt, black pepper and Tabasco, leaning heavily on Tabasco sauce to give sting. Add 2 cups water. Cook about 1/2 hour on medium fire or until well done. Add parsley and onion tops a few minutes before sauce is done. Serve over hot cooked rice along with tossed green salad or potato salad and hot garlic bread.

RACELAND

Clara B. Theriot
LAFOURCHE PARISH

Maw's Oyster Dressing
SERVES 14

2 lbs. ground beef
2 lbs. ground pork
2 pints oysters
2 raw sweet potatoes
1 large onion
3 stalks celery with tops
1 pack parsley
2 packs shallots

5 1 inch slices stale French
bread
3 large cooking spoons of
Mazola cooking oil
Salt
Paprika
Red and black pepper

Cut oysters (approximately 6 dozen) in small pieces and put back in water. Cut 3 stalks of celery, including top leaves, and chop fine. Cut stale bread in small pieces. Cut onion, shallots and parsley very fine. Peal and cut sweet potatoes in small pieces. In a large heavy pot put 3 large cooking spoons of Mazola oil and add ground meat and season with salt, pepper and paprika to taste. Cook until meat is brown. Add shallots, parsley, onions, sweet potatoes, celery and oysters with the water and cook. Stir as the seasonings are cooking, approximately 1 hour. Add chopped French bread and simmer on low fire until dressing is cooked and add additional seasoning to taste, approximately 45 minutes.

RESERVE
Mrs. Eola Boe Weber
ST. JOHN THE BAPTIST PARISH

Island Ham And Sweet Potatoes
SERVES 20

4 tbsp. butter
1 cup bell pepper strips
2 number 2 cans sliced pineapple OR
20 slices pineapple, drain and save juice
2 tbsp. cornstarch
4 tbsp. brown sugar
1 1/2 cups pineapple juice
4 tbsp. vinegar
3 16 oz. cans sweet potatoes, drained
2 sticks real butter, melted
1 tall can evaporated milk
Ham slices

Mix the 4 tbsp. butter, pineapple juice, cornstarch, brown
sugar, vinegar and heat until thickened. Remove from heat
and add bell pepper strips. In blender or mixer put sweet
potatoes, 2 sticks melted butter and add evaporated milk until
it is a smooth firm mixture that will stay mounded. Place
slices of ham in large casserole, lay a slice of pineapple on
top of each slice of ham. Heap sweet potatoes on top of
pineapple. Pour the sauce over all and heat uncovered at 350
degrees until bubbly. "It is the sweet and sour sauce that
makes it so good. Can be made ahead of time and
refrigerated."

ROSEDALE

Talma Gantt
IBERVILLE PARISH

Broccoli Rice Casserole

SERVES 10

2 cups cooked rice (not instant)
3 tbsp. butter
1 box frozen broccoli
1 cup onions, chopped
1 cup celery, chopped
1 can cream of chicken soup
1 can milk
1 small jar Cheez Whiz
Salt and pepper to taste

While broccoli is thawing in one cup of water that has been brought to a boil, saute' onions and celery in butter. Add soup and milk (use soup can as measure) to onions and celery. Add Cheez Whiz. Simmer for a minute or so, then add thawed broccoli and rice and seasoning. Bake 30 to 40 minutes in moderate oven. This can be made ahead of time.

SLAUGHTER
Lindsay A. Dawson
EAST FELICIANA PARISH

Bev's Corn Crab Soup

SERVES 6-8

1 cup onion, diced
1 cup green onion, diced
1 cup celery, diced
1 stick butter
2 pints Half N' Half cream
1 lb. crabmeat
1 can Niblets corn
Salt and pepper

Melt butter in large sauce pan. Add onion, green onion, celery and saute' in butter until onion is "clear", but not browned. Add corn, reduce heat slightly, and simmer for 10 minutes. Slowly stir in Half N' Half until all is mixed well. Simmer three or four minutes to regain heat (no need to if Half N' Half is at room temperature when added). Add crabmeat, simmer another ten minutes, then add salt and pepper to taste.

SLIDELL

Beverly B. Ferguson
ST. TAMMANY PARISH

Hog Cracklin
SERVES 15-20

40 lbs. fat from hog
1/2 to 1 gallon hog lard
Salt

Cut fat in 1/2 inch strips or 1 1/2 squares. Put in Number 15 or 20 washed black pot. Add lard and start to heat. When fat starts to fry cut fire down and fry for about 45 minutes or until small white blisters start to appear on skin. At this point take cracklin out and put on table to cool. When cool to touch, raise fire until lard gets 350 to 400 degrees. Put fat back in pot and stir until golden brown., Just before taking out sprinkle cool water 2 or 3 times. Take out before burning.

SORRENTO
Gilbert Melancon
ASCENSION PARISH

90

Sweet Potato Bread
MAKES 3 LOAVES

2 cups honey
1 cup cooking oil
3 eggs
3 1/2 cups whole wheat flour
2 tsp. baking soda
1/2 tsp. salt
1 tsp. cinnamon
1 tsp. nutmeg
2 1/2 cooked, mashed sweet potatoes
1 cup chopped pecans

Combine honey and oil and beat well. Add eggs and beat. Combine dry ingredients and add to wet mixture. You may add a little water 1/3 to 1/2 cup if needed to keep batter smooth. Stir in sweet potaotes and nuts. Pour into 3 small 6" X 3 1/2" X 2" well greased loaf pans. Bake at 350 degrees for 45 to 55 minutes. Freezes well.

ST. FRANCISVILLE
Karen Harrington
WEST FELICIANA PARISH

Italian Meatballs and Spaghetti Sauce

SERVES 10-12

SAUCE:
1 large onion, chopped
3 12 oz. cans tomato paste
2 8 oz. cans tomato sauce
10 to 12 cups hot water
6 pods garlic, finely chopped or
2 tsp. minced garlic
1/2 bell pepper, chopped
2 tsp. salt
1 tbsp. pepper
3/4 cup sugar
1 or 2 cans whole mushrooms

MEATBALLS:
3 lbs. lean ground beef
1 tsp. salt
1/4 tsp. black pepper
1/2 small onion, finely chopped
3 cloves garlic, finely chopped
2 eggs
1/2 cup seasoned bread crumbs or
1 slice wet bread
1/2 cup water

For SAUCE: Saute' onion in large Dutch oven in a small amount of oil over low heat. Add tomato paste and sauce. Simmer several minutes. Rinse out 5 cans with water and stir into mixture. Briskly stir for several minutes. Add hot water. Season with garlic, bell pepper, salt, black pepper, sugar and mushrooms, if desired. Cook slowly over low heat. After the sauce has cooked 2 1/2 to 3 hours, add meatballs. Cook and additional hour. If sauce cooks down too much, add hot water or more tomato sauce. Tailor sauce to taste.

MEATBALLS:
Place ground meat in large bowl. Add salt, pepper, onion, garlic, eggs and bread crumbs or bread. Mix by squeezing meat. Overmixing will make balls sticky. If mixture is dry, add 1/4 to 1/2 cups cold water. Roll meatballs about the size of a golf ball. Fry meatballs in small amount of oil. Brown on all sides, being careful not to burn. Remove and set aside.

ST. GABRIEL

Mrs. Frances Peltier
IBERVILLE PARISH

Shrimp Jambalaya
SERVES 6-8

2 lbs. peeled and deveined shrimp
4 cups cooked rice
2 tbsp. tomato paste
1 tsp. sugar
4 cloves garlic, minced
1 cup onions, chopped
2 cups water
1/2 cup celery and bell pepper, chopped
1/4 lb. oleo
1/2 tsp. flour
1/2 cup shallots and parsley, chopped fine
Tony Chachere's to taste

Cook rice separately. Chop shrimp and set aside. Melt oleo and add chopped onions, celery, bell pepper and garlic in a heavy pot. Cook uncovered over medium heat until onions are wilted. Add tomato paste and cook, stirring for about 15 minutes. Lower heat, if necessary, to avoid sticking. Add 1 1/2 cups water. Season to taste. Add sugar and cook uncovered over medium heat for about 40 minutes stirring occasionally or until oil floats to the top. Add shrimp and stir for another 20 minutes. Dissolve flour in 1/2 cup water and add. Cook another 5 minutes. Mix ingredients with cooked rice, add shallots and parsley. Mix again. This recipe can be doubled easily to feed a "hungry bunch".
"Good eating-La. style!"

THIBODAUX
Mary Alice Richard
LAFOURCHE PARISH

Roman Holiday
SERVES 8-10

1 1/2 to 2 lbs ground meat
1 large onion, chopped
1 lb. number 4 spaghetti
1 or 2 10 oz. cans Rotel tomatoes with green chilies
1 large can peas, drained (optional)
1 large box Velveeta cheese
Shredded cheddar cheese for topping

Brown ground meat and onion. Drain, leaving meat damp.
Boil spaghetti for 10 to 12 minutes, but not all the way. Do not
strain. Leave in water. Fork spaghetti into a large mixing
bowl. Add ground meat, tomatoes and peas. Mix together.
Pour and spread into casserole dish. Stick chunks of
Velveeta into mixture, down to bottom of dish and layer on
top. Sprinkle top with cheddar cheese. Bake uncovered at
350 degrees for 40 to 45 minutes or until brown. NOTE:
Chicken can be used in place of ground meat.

TICKFAW

Vickie Baiamonte
TANGIPAHOA PARISH

Peach Cobbler

SERVES 10

FILLING:
1 large cans sliced peaches and
1 regular sized can of peaches
2 cups sugar
2 to 4 tbsp. of all purpose flour
1/4 tsp. ground nutmeg
1/2 tsp. cinnamon
1 tsp. almond or vanilla extract
1/3 cup melted butter or margarine

PIE CRUST:
2 cups all purpose flour
2/3 cup Crisco
1 tsp. salt
6 tbsp. ice water
2 1/2 tsp. sugar

FILLING: Combine peaches with syrup in a large pot, add flour, nutmeg and cinnamon. Bring peaches to a boil, reduce heat, add extract and butter, stirring well until it thickens. Take off stove. DOUGH: In a bowl mix flour, salt and sugar, then Crisco. Stir with a fork until dough gets crumbly, then add ice water. Knead dough and make two equal balls. With rolling pin, flatten out dough. Cut into strips about 1 inch wide. Pour half of peaches evenly over 12 3/4" X 9" x 2" pan and lattice strips of dough over peaches. Bake at 350 degrees until dough is cooked. Pour remaining peaches over cooked dough, then lattice the other dough over peaches. Bake until dough is done.

VACHERIE
Mrs. Tonita W. Ricard
ST. JAMES PARISH

Wrapped Chicken Livers
SERVES 16

1 1/2 lbs. chicken livers
1/4 cup seasoned dry bread crumbs
1 tbsp. Parmesan cheese
1/2 tsp. basil
16 slices bacon, cut in half crosswise

Cut chicken livers into 1 1/4" pieces, making about 32 pieces. In small bowl, combine bread crumbs, cheese and basil. Coat livers with crumb mixture. Wrap a piece of bacon around each liver. Place on two 12 inch metal skewers, leaving a small space between livers. Place on rack in broiler pan. Broil 3 to 5 inches from heat source about 8 to 10 minutes on each side or until bacon is cooked through. Remove the meat from the skewers.

VARNADO
Mrs. Paris Sumrall
WASHINGTON PARISH

Ola's Shrimp Fettucine

SERVES 4-6

3 green onions, chopped
2 cups mushrooms, sliced
1 1/2 cloves garlic, minced
1 stick butter
2 tbsp. oil
1 lb. peeled shrimp
2 tsp. salt
8 oz. noodles
3/4 cup Romano cheese, grated
3/4 cup Parmesan cheese, grated
1 cup heavy cream
1/4 cup fresh parsley, chopped

In a large skillet, saute' onions, mushrooms and garlic in 1/2 stick butter and oil. Add shrimp and saute' until pink. Pour off excess liquid. Season with salt and cover to keep warm. Cook noodles in salted, boiling water. Drain. In saucepan melt remaining 1/2 stick butter. Add noodles, cheeses and cream. Mix well and combine with shrimp mixture. Sprinkle with parsley, toss and serve.

VIOLET

Viola T. Dufrene
ST. BERNARD PARISH

Pecan Pralines
MAKES 2 DOZEN

2 cups sugar
1 cup Pet milk
2 cups chopped pecans
4 tbsp. butter or margarine
Dash of vanilla

Dissolve sugar in pet milk and bring to a boil, stirring
occasionally. Add the butter and pecans. Cook until syrup
reaches the soft ball stage or 280 degrees. Test in cold water.
Cool 10 minutes without disturbing. Add vanilla. Beat until
thick. Drop by spoonful on aluminium foil.

WESTWEGO

Annie B. Guidry
JEFFERSON PARISH

Crawfish Tortellini

SERVES 4-6

7 oz. Parmesan cheese Tortellini, plain or spinach
1 stick butter
1 medium onion, finely chopped
1 pod garlic, finely chopped
1/4 to 1/2 cup Parmesan cheese
Whipping cream
1 lb. crawfish tails
1/8 cup parsley, chopped
Salt and pepper
Red pepper
Tony Chachere's seasoning

Saute' onions and garlic in butter. Add crawfish and cook on low for 5 minutes. Stir in Parmesan cheese, parsley and enough whipping cream to create a heavy sauce. Fold prepared tortellini into crawfish mixture. Season to taste.

WHITE CASTLE

Kay Russell
IBERVILLE PARISH

Crabmeat Au Gratin

SERVES 4-6

1 lb. crabmeat
2 egg yolks
2 cans of Pet Milk
2 cups onions, chopped
1 stick butter
1/2 cup celery, chopped
1/2 cup flour
1/2 tsp. black pepper
1/2 tsp. red pepper
1 tsp. salt

Saute' onions, celery, pepper and salt in butter. Add flour, milk and egg yolks. Reduce heat and cook for 5 minutes. Add mixture to crabmeat. Can be poured into individual dishes. Add cheese on top when ready to serve.

WHITEHALL

Wilta Ann Edwards
LIVINGSTON PARISH

Broccoli Casserole
SERVES 6

1 package chopped frozen broccoli
1 jar Cheez Whiz
1 can cream of mushroom soup
1 cup cooked rice
1 tsp. salt
1 small onion, chopped
1 tbsp. margarine

Melt margarine in a large skillet. Add chopped onions and
saute' until tender. Add chopped unthawed broccoli and cover
for about 10 minutes. Add soup, rice and Cheez Whiz. Stir
until well mixed. Pour in casserole dish and bake at 400
degrees for about 15 minutes.

WILSON
Linda Barrett
EAST FELICIANA PARISH

Lemon Baked Chicken
SERVES 12

3 tbsp. lemon rind
3/4 cup lemon juice
3/4 cup water
3/4 cup corn oil
3 cloves garlic, minced
3 tbsp. soy sauce
1 1/2 cups flour
3 2 1/2 to 3 1/2 lb. fryers, cut up
3 tsp. salt
3 tsp. pepper
2 tbsp. paprika

Mix together lemon rind and juice, water, corn oil, soy sauce, garlic, 1 tsp. each of salt and pepper. Pour over chicken, cover and refrigerate at least 3 hours or overnight. Drain chicken on absorbent paper, reserving marinade. Mix together flour, paprika and remaining salt and pepper. Coat chicken. Shake off excess. Place skin side down in 2 shallow pans. Bake at 400 degrees for 30 minutes. Turn chicken. Pour marinade over chicken and bake 30 minutes longer, basting occasionally.

ZACHARY

Mae Dee C. Landry
EAST BATON ROUGE PARISH

Southwest Section

Abbeville	Jennings
Amelia	Kaplan
Baldwin	Lafayette
Berwick	Lake Arthur
Breaux Bridge	Lake Charles
Broussard	Loreauville
Cameron	Mermentau
Carencro	Morgan City
Church Point	Morse
Crowley	New Iberia
Delcambre	Parks
DeQuincy	Patterson
Duson	Rayne
Elton	Roanoke
Erath	Scott
Franklin	St. Martinville
Garden City	Sulphur
Gueydan	Vinton
Iota	Welsh
Iowa	Westlake
Jeanerette	Youngsville

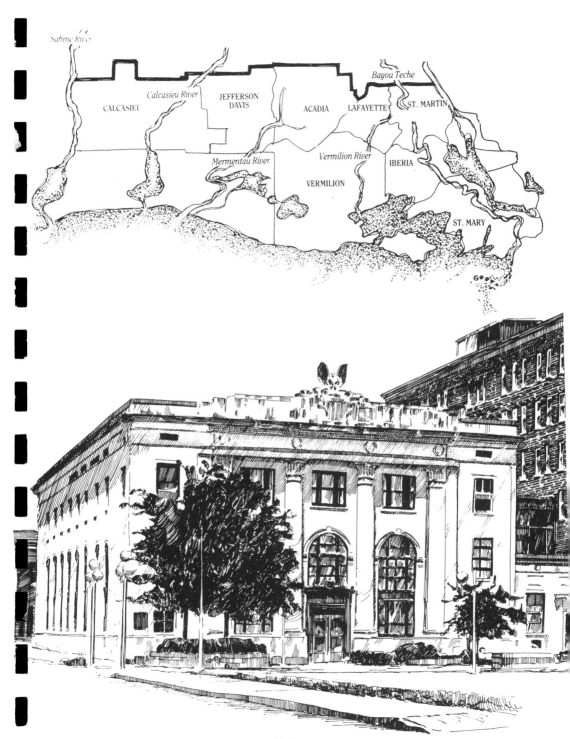

Oven-Baked Chicken Fricasse'
SERVES 6

1 fryer
1 pkg. dry onion soup
1 can cream of mushroom soup
1 onion
1/4 cup green parsley
3/4 can water
1 tbsp. Kitchen Bouquet

3/4 bell pepper
2 stems celery
1/4 cup green onions
1/4 tsp. salt
1/4 tsp. back pepper
1/4 tsp. red pepper
1 clove of garlic chopped or
1 tbsp. garlic powder

Season fryer (cut-up) in the pan sprayed with Pam to be used in the oven. Mix together the following: dry onion soup, mushroom soup, Kitchen Bouquet and 3/4 cup of water. Pour this over the chicken parts in the pan. Sprinkle in the chopped onion, celery and bell pepper and spread around. Preheat oven to 375 degrees. Bake this mixture for about 1 1/2 hours (with cover). About 1/2 hour before finish, sprinkle in the chopped green onions and parsley. Serve over rice.

ABBEVILLE

Carolyn D. Songne'
VERMILION PARISH

Shrimp With Sausage BBQ Sauce
SERVES 8-10

3 lbs. peeled/deveined shrimp
1 smoked sausage link,
chopped fine
1/2 stick butter
1 1/2 cup onion, chopped
1 cup white port wine
1 1/2 cup Tony Chachere
BBQ Sauce
1 tbsp. Tabasco
Salt and pepper to taste
French bread if desired

Melt butter in a large saucepan (6 qt.). Add sausage,
slightly brown; add onions and cook until clear; then add the
shrimp and cook on med/low heat until shrimp become heated
thoroughly; add wine, BBQ sauce and Tabasco; cook on low
heat, stirring occasionally. Add salt and pepper if needed.
Cook until tender or about 1 hour. Great with fresh French
bread. Serves 8-10 regular people or 4-6 Cajuns.

AMELIA

Carol Benoit
ST. MARY PARISH

Superior Chicken And Broccoli
SERVES 6

1 medium chicken
1 stick margarine
1 large onion, chopped
1 can cream of celery soup
1 can cream of chicken soup
1 small Velveeta
1 box frozen broccoli, chopped
1 package #4 spaghetti
Salt
Red pepper

Boil chicken for 1 hour, debone, chop and set aside. Boil spaghetti in broth and set aside. Saute' onion in margarine, add both soups and cheese, cook 10 minutes. Add chopped chicken, simmer 10 minutes. Add cooked, drained broccoli. Salt and pepper to taste and simmer 10 minutes. Add cooked spaghetti, mix well and enjoy!

BALDWIN
Gerry Darce
ST. MARY PARISH

Crawfish Pie

SERVES 4

2 lb. peeled crawfish tails
1/4 lb. oleo
1/2 cup celery, chopped
1 cup onions, chopped
1/2 cup bell pepper, chopped
2 tbsp. cornstarch
4 cloves garlic, minced
2 cups cold water
1/4 cup onion tops, chopped
1/4 cup parsley, chopped
Salt, pepper and cayenne to taste
1 pie shell

Season crawfish tails with seasonings and set aside. Melt oleo in a heavy pot. Add onions, bell pepper, garlic, and celery; cook until onions are wilted, stirring constantly. Add 1 1/2 cups of water and crawfish tails. Bring to a boil and cook over slow heat for 30 minutes, stirring constantly. Pour into a raw pie shell. Cover top of pie with rolled pie dough. Pinch edges together. Cut slits in top. Bake in 350 degree oven till crust is done, approximately 1 hour.

BERWICK

Glynda Lasseigne
ST. MARY PARISH

Crawfish Etouffee
SERVES 6 TO 8

1-2 lbs. crawfish tails
1 stick margarine
2 onions, chopped
1 bell pepper, chopped
2 ribs celery, chopped
1/2 clove garlic
2 cans tomato sauce
1 can golden mushroom soup

1 can Rotel tomatoes
3 cups water
1/2 cup green onion tops, chopped
2 tbsp. parsley
Salt
Pepper
Garlic powder

Melt margarine in dutch oven. Add chopped onions, bell pepper, celery and garlic. Saute' until light brown. Add tomato sauce, mushroom soup, Rotel tomatoes and water. Salt, pepper and garlic powder to taste. Cook over low heat 1 1/2 to 2 hours stirring often to keep from sticking. Then add crawfish, green onions and parsley. Cook another 20 minutes. Serve over rice.

BREAUX BRIDGE

Frances Randall

ST MARTIN PARISH

110

Shrimp Marguerite
SERVES 6-8

1 stick butter or oleo
1 1/4 cup onions, chopped
1 bell pepper, chopped
2 pods garlic, chopped
2 stalks celery, chopped
1/2 cup water
1 can Rotel tomatoes, chopped
3 cups raw, peeled shrimp (cut in half)
1 can cream of mushroom soup
1/4 cup pimento, chopped
4 slices bread
1/4 cup parsley, chopped
2 cups cooked rice
Bread crumbs

Saute' chopped seasonings in the butter. Add shrimp and Rotel tomatoes. Cook together for 5 minutes. Add mushroom soup, water and pimento. Cook for 5 min. more. Soak bread slices in water to cover. Squeeze all water from bread. Add to shrimp mixture (break apart with spoon as you stir). Add 2 cups cooked rice and parsley. Pour into greased casserole and cover with bread crumbs. Bake 1/2 hour at 450 degrees.

BROUSSARD

Mrs. Marguerite Blue
LAFAYETTE PARISH

Crawfish Janie
SERVES 4

1 medium onion, chopped
2 stalks celery, chopped
1/2 medium green pepper, chopped
1 lb. crawfish, peeled and cleaned
1 can cream of mushroom soup
1 can diced Rotel tomatoes and chilis
1/4 stick butter
1 lb. Velveeta cheese
1 lb. Rotini macaroni, cooked
Salt to taste

Saute' chopped onion, celery, green pepper in butter. Melt the cheese and mix with vegetables and remaining ingredients. Pour mixture into a large casserole and bake at 350 degrees for 35 to 40 minutes.

CAMERON
Mrs. Janie Fulton Turnbull
CAMERON PARISH

Eggplant Dressing
SERVES 10

4 medium eggplant
3 medium onions, sliced
1 1/2 cups celery, chopped
3 tbsp. oil
1 1/2 lb. ground beef
1 1/2 lb. ground pork
3 cups water
1/2 cup bell pepper, chopped
1/2 cup green onion, chopped
4 cups cooked rice
1/2 cup parsley, chopped
Salt, black and red pepper to taste

Peel and chop eggplant; set aside. Lightly brown beef and pork in oil. Add eggplant, onions and celery and smother covered on medium heat. Stir until all ingredients are brown. (If it sticks, add a little water). When brown, add 3 cups of water. Add bell pepper, green onions and parsley. Cook on low heat for 30 to 40 minutes. Mix in rice and simmer covered for 15 to 20 minutes more, stirring occasionally. Great for large family gatherings.

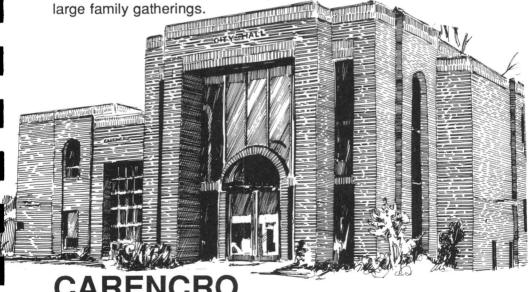

CARENCRO
Mrs. Vivian L. Hebert
LAFAYETTE PARISH

Shrimp Creole

SERVES 6-8

1/4 cup oil
1/4 cup flour
1 cup onions, chopped
1/4 cup celery, chopped
1 8 oz. can tomato sauce
2 lb. cleaned shrimp
1/4 cup dry sherry wine (optional)
3 tbsp. green onions, chopped
3 tbsp. parsley, chopped
2 tsp. salt
1/2 tsp. black pepper (optional)
1/2 tsp. red pepper

Make golden roux with flour and oil (color of peanut butter).
Add onions and celery and cook until clear, about 10 minutes.
Add tomato sauce and cook 10 minutes. Add raw shrimp.
Cook 10 minutes. Add dry sherry wine, green onions and
cook 10 minutes. Add parsley - If too thick, add 1 can (tomato
sauce can) of water. Serve hot over rice.

CHURCH POINT

Anita G. Guidry
ACADIA PARISH

Crawfish Etouffee
SERVES 4

1 stick butter
1/2 cup celery, chopped
1/2 can water
1 large onion, chopped
1/4 cup beer
1 cup cream of mushroom soup
1/2 bell pepper, chopped
1 can Rotel tomatoes
1 lb. peeled crawfish tails
Salt and red pepper to taste

Melt butter in large pot on low heat. Then add onions, celery and bell pepper. Saute' for 10 minutes. Add water, beer and cream of mushroom soup and Rotel tomatoes. Stir and mix well. Then add crawfish tails. Add seasonings, cover pot and cook for 20 minutes on low heat. Stir occasionally. Serve with rice.

CROWLEY

Helen Zaunbrecher/Billie Jennings/Sandra Henry
ACADIA PARISH

115

Shrimp Fettucine

SERVES 10-12

3 lbs. peeled shrimp
3 sticks oleo
3 onions, chopped
3 bell peppers, chopped
3 stalks celery, chopped
4-6 pods garlic, chopped
1/4 cup flour
1 pint Half N' Half cream
1 lb. jalapeno cheese
1 lb. fettucine noodles
Grated cheese
Parmesan cheese
Season to taste

Saute' onions, bell peppers, celery in margarine. Add parsley, garlic and shrimp and cook for 10 minutes. Add cream, cheese and flour. Simmer for 1/2 hour. Boil and drain noodles, stir well. Pour mixture in a large casserole dish and top with grated cheese and Parmesan cheese. Bake at 350 degrees for 20 minutes.

DELCAMBRE

Patti L. Vincent
VERMILION PARISH

Beef Ranchero

SERVES 6

1 large onion, diced
1 large green pepper, diced
2 stalks celery, diced
1 lb. lean hamburger
2 cups canned tomatoes
1/2 cup uncooked rice
2 tbsp. cooking oil
2 tsp. salt
1 tsp. chili powder
1/4 tsp. black pepper

Cook onions, pepper and celery in cooking oil until onions are yellow. Add meat and fry until mixture falls apart. Add tomatoes, rice, seasonings and mix well. Place in 2 quart greased casserole dish, cover and bake in a moderately hot oven (375 degrees) for 45 minutes or until done. Remove cover for last 10 minutes to brown top. May also be cooked over low heat on top of the stove. (One can tomato paste and 1 cup water may be substituted for tomatoes).

DEQUINCY

Mrs Woodrow A. Martin
CALCASIEU PARISH

Crawfish Spaghetti
SERVES 6

1 large onion, chopped
1 large bell pepper, chopped
1 10 3/4 oz. can of cream of
  mushroom soup
1 lb. peeled crawfish (with or
  without tail fat)
12 ozs. of very thin spaghetti
6 tbsp. margarine
1/4 cup of water
Konriko Creole Seasoning

Saute' chopped onion and bell pepper in margarine on medium heat for about 35-40 minutes. Lower heat. Add cream of mushroom soup and simmer for 45 minutes, stirring occasionally. Add 1/4 cup water, crawfish and season to taste. Cook for 20-25 minutes. While crawfish is cooking, boil spaghetti. In large bowl mix crawfish and spaghetti. Great with green salad.

DUSON

Connie Hanks
LAFAYETTE PARISH

Eggplant Deborah
SERVES 8-10

2 large eggplants, 1 peeled, both cut into fourths
Water to cover eggplants
1 tsp. salt
4 strips bacon, chopped
1 stick unsalted butter
1 large onion, chopped
1 medium bell pepper, chopped
1 stalk celery, diced
1/2 tsp. Tabasco sauce
1/4 tsp. garlic powder
1/2 tsp. onion powder
1 tsp. lemon juice
2 1/2 cups Ritz cracker crumbs
Salt and pepper to taste
1/4 cup plain bread crumbs
2 pats butter, cut into pieces
1 lb. shrimp

Preheat oven to 350 degrees. Place eggplant in a large sauce pan and cover with water. Add salt and bring water to a boil over high heat. Boil for 1 minute then turn off the heat. Let the eggplant sit in the water until you are ready to use it. In another large saucepan or skillet, saute' the bacon until it is brown and crisp. Melt butter in the saucepan with the bacon, then add the onion, bell pepper and celery. Saute' for four minutes over medium heat or until the onions are clear. Remove eggplant from the water with a slotted spoon (do not worry about draining all the water) and place it in the skillet. Also add the shrimp. Saute' for 5 minutes. Season with Tabasco sauce, garlic powder, onion powder and lemon juice. Blend in the cracker crumbs and salt and pepper to taste. Pour into a casserole dish. Sprinkle lightly with the bread crumbs and dot with butter. Bake at 350 degrees for 30 minutes.

ELTON

Kitty Marsh
JEFFERSON DAVIS PARISH

Hitachi Crawfish Jambalaya

SERVES 8 TO 10

1 lb. crawfish tails
1 large bell pepper, chopped
2 cups raw rice (use rice measure
   from cooker)
1 stick margarine
2 stalks celery, chopped
1 large onion, chopped
1 10 3/4 oz. can chicken broth
Red pepper and salt to taste

Chop onion, bell pepper and celery stalks. Place in rice cooker pot. Add rest of ingredients and stir to mix. Adjust seasoning to your personal taste. Plug in Hitachi Rice Cooker and cook covered about 30 minutes. Stir once when mixture is boiling. PLEASE NOTE: Shrimp, crab meat or Lobster may be used instead of crawfish.

ERATH

Terry L. Lancon
VERMILION PARISH

Louisiana Yam Casserole
SERVES 6-8

5 cups Louisiana cooked yams
2 large eggs
1 tsp. salt
1 1/2 cups sugar
1/2 cup flour
1 1/2 tsp. vanilla
1/2 tsp. cinnamon
1/2 tsp. nutmeg
1 1/2 sticks butter or margarine
1/2 cup brown sugar
1/2 cup pecans, chopped

Combine all ingredients until blended smoothly. Pour into
greased dish. Bake at 350 degrees for 25 minutes.

FRANKLIN

Anne Lobdell Blackman
ST. MARY PARISH

Pork Chop And Turnip Stew
SERVES 10

10 pork chops
4 large turnips, sliced thin
1 tbsp. flour
1/2 cup cooking oil
1 large onion, diced
Garlic salt
Salt
Pepper

Brown pork chops well in hot oil. Add flour and onion. Add water to cover chops. Bring to a boil, then simmer for 45 minutes. Add sliced turnips and simmer for 30 minutes.

GARDEN CITY

Sherry Luke
ST. MARY PARISH

Sausage Jambalaya
SERVES 4

1 lb. hot smoked sausage
2 cups rice
1 no. 2 can tomatoes
1/2 cup celery, diced
1 large onion, diced
1/2 cup green onions, chopped
1/2 cup parsley, chopped
5 cloves garlic, diced
1/2 tsp. red pepper
1 tsp. salt

Combine tomatoes (you can use stewed tomatoes), seasonings and cut pieces of cooked smoked sausage. Mix cooked rice into gravy with fork. Do not stir. Add 1/2 cup chopped green onions and 1/2 cup chopped parsley. Cook on low fire for 10 minutes.

GUEYDAN

Gracie Guidry
VERMILION PARISH

Rice Dressing
SERVES 6

1 lb. ground lean meat
1 big onion, chopped
1 bell pepper, chopped
2 pieces celery, chopped
1/4 cup cooking oil
1/4 cup parsley, minced
1/4 cup green onion tops, chopped
2 tsp. salt
1/2 tsp. red pepper
1/2 tsp. thyme leaves
1 bay leaf
2 cups water
6 cups cooked rice

Brown meat in oil, add onions, bell pepper and celery. Cook till seasoning is limp, stirring all the while. Add salt, pepper, thyme, bay leaf and water. Simmer for 30 minutes on low fire. Discard bay leaf. Mix well with rice, green onion tops and parsley. Cover and let stand for 10 minutes before serving.

IOTA

Lucille Gravot
ACADIA PARISH

Pride Of The Gulf
SERVES 8

1 pint crabmeat	Bell pepper
1-1 1/2 lbs. shrimp	Onion
8 oz. cream cheese	Parsley
1 1/2 cups cooked rice	Green onion
1 can cream of mushroom	Touch of garlic salt
soup	Tabasco sauce to taste
1 stick of margarine	Salt to taste
Cheddar cheese	Black pepper to taste

Saute' onions, bell pepper, parsley and green onions in butter. Add shrimp and saute'. Add soup and cream cheese, crab meat and rice. Mix well, pour into casserole dish and top with cheddar cheese. Microwave for 10-20 minutes or bake in moderate oven for 30 minutes. Serve hot.

IOWA

Genevieve Franklin
CALCASIEU PARISH

Crawfish Fettucini Casserole

SERVES 10-12

3 onions, chopped
3 celery stalks, chopped
2 bell peppers, chopped
2 buttons garlic
3 sticks oleo
1/4 cup flour
4 tbsp. dried parsley

1 pint cream, Half n' Half
1 lb. Velveeta
1 lb fettucini noodles, boiled "Al Dente"
2 tbsp. jalapenos
3 lbs. crawfish, peeled
Parmesan cheese
Salt and pepper to taste

Saute' first seven ingredients together for 15 minutes. Stir often. Add crawfish. Cook 15 minutes. Stir often. Add Half n' Half and 1/2 of Velveeta and all jalapenos. Add salt and pepper and cook for 30 minutes. Stir often. Add cooked noodles. Put in greased casserole dish. Top with Parmesan and remaining Velveeta. Bake 350 degrees for 15 to 20 minutes. NOTE: Shrimp may be substituted for crawfish.

JEANERETTE

Gayle Clement
IBERIA PARISH

Dr. Jackie's Glazed Pork Loin Roast
SERVES 20-25

2 5 to 6 lb. pork loin roasts, deboned
1 lb. Jimmy Dean Hot bulk sausage
1 lb. Jimmy Dean Mild bulk sausage
1/2 cup onions, chopped
1 cup seasoned bread crumbs
8 oz. dried apricots, chopped
Salt
White pepper
Marjoram
Garlic powder
1 8 oz. jar apricot preserves
1/2 cup cooking sherry

Mix sausages, onion, chopped dried apricots, bread crumbs and a small amount of salt. Stuff between the two roasts and tie with string. Season roasts to taste, cover with foil and bake at 250 degrees for 1 hour and 45 minutes. (GLAZE: 1 8 oz. jar apricot preserves and 1/2 cup cooking sherry) Mix apricot preserves and sherry and glaze roast and bake for 1 1/2 to 2 hours more at 350 degrees.

JENNINGS
Dolores Spears
JEFFERSON DAVIS PARISH

Microwave Shrimp And Crawfish Casserole

SERVES 20

1 lb. raw shrimp
1 lb. raw crawfish
1 cup onions, chopped
1 cup bell pepper, chopped
1/2 cup celery, chopped
1/2 stick of margarine
1 1/2 cans cream of mushroom soup
5-6 cups of cooked rice

Saute' onions, celery and bell pepper in the 1/2 stick of margarine using a 2 quart covered casserole dish. Add shrimp and crawfish and saute' for 5 minutes. Mix in cream of mushroom soup and cooked rice. Mix well. Cook covered in microwave on high for 8-12 minutes. Mix gently 2 or 3 times during cooking time.

KAPLAN

Gayle Bourque
VERMILION PARISH

Cajun's Ragin Casserole
SERVES 8

2 packages frozen spinach, chopped
4 tbsp. butter
2 tbsp. flour
1/2 cup Pet milk
2 tbsp. onion, chopped
1/2 cup spinach liquid
6 oz. jalapeno cheese roll
3/4 tsp. celery salt
3/4 tsp. garlic powder (no added salt)
1 tbsp. Worcestershire sauce
Cajun liquid - hot pepper sauce to taste
Buttered bread crumbs

Cook spinach according to package, drain and save liquid.
Melt butter. Stir in flour. Add onion. Add liquids (Pet milk and
spinach juice). Cook on low heat, till smooth and thick, stirring
constantly. Add seasonings and cheese, which has been cut
into small pieces. When melted, combine with cooked spinach. Pour into casserole dish, top with buttered bread crumbs
and bake in 325 degree oven until hot and crumbs brown.
Can be frozen. (Flavor improves over night).

LAFAYETTE

Joy M. Sonnier
LAFAYETTE PARISH

Strawberry Delight
SERVES 6-8

1 large box strawberry Jello (family size)
2 10 oz. cans frozen strawberries, thawed
3 bananas, mashed
1 large can crushed pineapples, drained
1 cup pecans, chopped
1 pint sour cream

Dissolve Jello in 2 cups boiling water. Add strawberries,
bananas, pineapple and pecans. Pour 1/2 of mixture in a 3" x
6" dish and place in freezer to set. After mixture has set, layer
sour cream on top and then pour in remaining mixture and
chill overnight.

LAKE ARTHUR

Katy Brunt
JEFFERSON DAVIS PARISH

Cajun Ratatouille
SERVES 8-10

3 cloves garlic (real Cajuns like more)
3/4 cups olive oil
1 lb. (6 med.) zucchini
3 large green bell peppers
3 large red bell peppers
1 lb. eggplant or 2 large eggplants
2 large tomatoes (canned can be used)
1 large onion (more if you like)
Salt to taste
Cayenne pepper to taste
1 tbsp. sweet basil
1 or 2 bay leaves
1/2 tsp. black pepper
1 chicken bouillon cube or stock (1/2 can)

To prepare vegetables for saute'ing, slice zucchini into 1/4 pieces, cut green and red peppers into 1/4 inch wide strips, slice onions thinly, cut peeled eggplant in 1 inch cubes and peel and quarter tomatoes. In heavy pot or skillet heat 1/4 cup of olive oil. Add garlic, zucchini and green and red peppers. Saute' 5 minutes, stirring gently. Remove to a bowl. Add additional 1/4 cup of olive oil, saute' onions and eggplant for 5 minutes stirring gently. Add to zucchini mixture. Add final 1/4 cup of olive oil and saute' tomatoes for 2 minutes. Turn all vegetables into skillet and add spices, herbs, salt and peppers. Stir gently and let simmer until vegetables seem slightly crisp but cooked. Add chicken broth. Can be served cold or hot. Garnish with fresh parsley and fresh basil.

LAKE CHARLES
Marilyn Cox
CALCASIEU PARISH

Real Cajun Fried Turkey

SERVES 6-8

1 large (12 lb.) turkey
Salt
Cayenne pepper
1 onion, chopped
1/2 stalk celery, chopped
5 gallons peanut oil

Season turkey inside and out with salt and cayenne pepper, using generous amounts. Stuff cavity with onion and celery. To keep onion and celery contained inside, sew cavity skin closed with string. Using a 60 quart pot, with outdoor burner, bring peanut oil to a boil. Gently place turkey in hot oil and cook for 4 to 5 minutes per pound. Remove and drain. Season to taste.

LOREAUVILLE

Tim Edler
IBERIA PARISH

Shrimp Etouffee

SERVES 8-10

2 lbs. cleaned shrimp	2 tbsp. cornstarch
2 sticks butter	2 cups water
3 large onions	1 tbsp. garlic, chopped
1 medium bell pepper	salt
3 ribs celery, chopped	pepper
1 can cream of mushroom	paprika
soup	1/2 cup onion tops

Season shrimp to taste. Melt butter and add the onions, bell pepper, celery and garlic. Cook until wilted. Add cream of mushroom soup. Mix well and simmer a few minutes. Then add shrimp and 1 1/2 cups of water and cook about 20 to 25 minutes or until shrimp are done. thicken gravy with cornstarch and 1/2 cup of water. Season with salt and pepper an add paprika for color. Then add onion tops. Serve hot over rice.

MERMENTAU

Mr. and Mrs. Warren Guidry
ACADIA PARISH

133

Crayfish Or Shrimp Fettuccini
SERVES 8

2 medium onions, chopped
3 green onions, chopped
1 medium bell pepper, chopped
2 celery sticks, chopped
1 1/2 sticks margarine
1 tbsp. flour
1/2 lb. Velveeta cheese

2 lbs. crayfish or shrimp, peeled
1/2 pint Half n' Half
1 tsp. parsley
1/2 cup jalapeno relish
3 cloves garlic
1/2 lb. fettuccini noodles
Parmesan cheese

Saute' vegetables in margarine until soft. Add flour, parsley and crayfish or shrimp. Cook for 15 minutes. Add relish, Velveeta cheese, Half n' Half and garlic. Cook for 15 minutes. Cook noodles. Fold noodles and crayfish or shrimp mixture. Cover with Parmesan cheese. Bake in 9" x 13" X 2" dish at 350 degrees for 15 minutes.

MORGAN CITY

Mrs. C.R. Brownell, Jr.
ST. MARY PARISH

Sausage Potato Stew

SERVES 6

1 onion, diced
2 lbs. smoked sausage
10 large potatoes, cubed
6 cups water
Rice
Black pepper
Salt
Dry parsley flakes

Cut sausage into 1 inch pieces. Put in large pot with 1 cup of water and boil until water evaporates and sausage browns in its own grease. Add 1 cup chopped onion and saute' 1 or 2 minutes. Add cubed potatoes with 5 cups water. Bring to a boil then reduce heat. Season with salt, pepper and parsley flakes to taste. Cover and simmer for about 45 minutes or until potatoes are tender. Serve over cooked rice.

MORSE

Kayla B. Schexnayder
ACADIA PARISH

Howard & Lorraine's
Supper Club Seafood Gumbo
SERVES 16

1 gallon oysters
10 lbs. medium shrimp
3 lbs. crabmeat
4 onions, chopped
2 bell pepper, chopped
1 cup celery, chopped
1 garlic pod, chopped
1 cup green onion, chopped
File'

1/2 cup parsley, chopped
1 quart water or seafood stock
1 bottle Tabasco Bloody Mary Mix
Tony's seasoning
1 tsp. thyme
1 tsp. oregano

Make a roux, when dark enough added chopped vegetables. Saute' until clear. Add water or seafood stock. Bring to boil and add Tabasco Bloody Mary Mix and oyster Liquor. Lower heat and simmer 2 - 2 1/2 hours. Add shrimp and crab meat 1 hour before serving. Add oysters 1/2 hour before serving and add seasonings. Add onion tops, parsley and file' last. Serve on rice with hot French bread.

NEW IBERIA
Howard and Lorraine Kingston
IBERIA PARISH

Chicken Tettrazini

SERVES 6

1 whole fryer, boiled and
deboned
1 lb. #4 spaghetti
1 can cream of chicken soup
6 oz. milk
1/4 cup pimento, diced
1/4 cup of green pepper,
chopped
1 tbsp. onion, minced
1 lb. Velveeta cheese
Salt and pepper to taste

Boil chicken and debone. Boil and drain spaghetti. Add
chicken and all other ingredients. Mix well and bake for 1
hour at 350 degrees.

PARKS

Mrs. Shelton LeBlanc
ST. MARTIN PARISH

Grandmother's Pound Cake

SERVES 12

1 cup butter
1 2/3 cups sugar
5 eggs
2 cups flour

Cream butter and sugar until light and fluffy. Beat in sugar and eggs, one at a time. When creamy add flour. Bake in greased and floured tube pan for 1 hour in slow 300 degree oven. Excellent for electric beater.

PATTERSON

Clara Bell Marin
ST. MARY PARISH

Cajun Pork Chop Rice
SERVES 4

Pork chops (1 or 2 per serving)
1 green pepper, chopped
1 or 2 onions, chopped
1 3 oz. can sliced mushrooms
Worcestershire sauce
1 cup rice
1 can whole tomatoes (Rotel)
Salt
Accent
Pepper

Season chops with salt, pepper and Accent. Brown chops over medium heat. Remove all fat left in skillet and remove from fire. Sprinkle over chops, uncooked rice, tomatoes, mushrooms (drained), chopped onions and green peppers. Add Worcestershire sauce to taste. Cook covered over low heat for 45 minutes.

RAYNE

Fair C. King
ACADIA PARISH

Shrimp And Crab Casserole
SERVES 6-8

1/2 cup celery, diced
1/2 cup onion, diced
1/2 cup bell pepper, diced
1/4 cup salad oil
1 can Rotel tomatoes
1 can cream of mushroom soup
1 can sliced mushrooms
1 lb. crabmeat

2 lbs. boiled shrimp
2 cups cooked rice
1 tbsp. Worcestershire sauce
1/4 tsp. paprika
Green onions, chopped
Parsley

Saute' celery, onions and bell pepper in salad oil. Add Rotel tomatoes, cream of mushroom soup, sliced mushrooms and simmer for 5 minutes. Add rest of ingredients, season to taste and place in casserole dish. Sprinkle with buttered bread crumbs and bake in 350 degree oven for 25 minutes.

ROANOKE

Dolores A. Miers
JEFFERSON DAVIS PARISH

Ole Tyme Fig Cookies
MAKES 7-8 DOZEN

2 cups sugar
2 eggs
1/2 cup shortening (butter flavor Crisco)
3 1/2 cups flour
1 tsp. baking soda
1 tsp. vanilla flavor
1/2 tsp. nutmeg
1/2 tsp. cinnamon
1 cup fig preserves
1 cup pecans, chopped

Cream sugar, eggs and shortening until creamy. Add the rest of the ingredients. Drop by teaspoonfull far apart on a greased cookie sheet. Bake at 350 degrees until light brown. "You can use more spices (to taste). I use a pint of fig preserves (mash if whole). If preserves have a lot of juice, you may have to add a little at a time. Happy eating!"

SCOTT

Lucille B. Domingue
LAFAYETTE PARISH

Southern Apple Pecan Cake
SERVES 8

4 cups finely chopped apples
2 cups sugar
2 1/2 cups flour
1/2 tsp. ginger
2 tsp. soda
1 cup cooking oil
1 tsp. salt
1 tsp. cinnamon
2 eggs
1 cup pecans, chopped

Let apples and 2 cups of sugar stand for half an hour or so.
Sift dry ingredients together in a large mixing bowl. Beat egg
whites until stiff. Beat egg yolks separately. Add cooking oil
to dry ingredients, mix well. Add apples and sugar. Add egg
whites and yolks. Mix well and put in tube pan. Bake at 350
degrees for 1 hour or until inserted toothpick comes clean.
"This is a long time favorite of my family. To make yours truly
Southern, substitute apples, nuts, raisins, for whatever fruits
are in season. Makes a nice holiday fruitcake".

ST MARTINVILLE
Thelma Domingue
ST. MARTIN PARISH

One Dish Supper

SERVES 6-8

1 1/2 lbs. ground beef, uncooked
1 1/2 lbs. smoked sausage, cut into pieces
3 cups uncooked rice
1 small head cabbage, shredded
1 large onion, diced
1 medium bell pepper, diced
2 cans Rotel tomatoes, diced
2 pods garlic, minced
2 cups water
3 tsp. salt
Pepper to taste

Combine all ingredients in large pot. Mix well. Bring to boil over medium heat. Do not stir rice after it starts to boil. Once mixture boils, cover with tight fitting lid, reduce heat and simmer for 30 to 35 minutes. Fluff with fork before serving. Serve with salad and French bread.

SULPHUR

Rita D. Prewitt
CALCASIEU PARISH

Pecan Surprise

SERVES 8

1 box yellow cake mix
1/2 cup melted butter
4 eggs
1 1/2 cups pecans
1/2 cup brown sugar
1 1/2 cup Karo syrup
1 tsp. vanilla

Mix 1/3 cup of cake mix, 1/2 cup of melted butter and one egg. Press down in 9" x 13" cake pan and bake at 350 degrees for 15 to 20 minutes. Mix other 2/3 cup cake mix, 1/2 cup brown sugar, 1 1/2 cups Karo syrup, 3 eggs and 1 tsp. of vanilla. Pour over top of first baked part and top with pecans. Return to oven and bake at 350 degrees for 30 to 35 minutes.

VINTON

Dorothy Smith
CALCASIEU PARISH

Oriental Shrimp And Vegetables
SERVES 10

1 1/2 lbs. cleaned shrimp
2 10 oz. packages Birdseye frozen stir fry
Japanese style vegetables
2 10 oz. packages Birdseye frozen
oriental style vegetables
1 1/2 cups water
1 stick of butter
1 or 2 tbsp. corn starch
2 packets stir fry seasoning mix
Salt and red pepper to taste
Soy sauce if desired

In large bowl empty packages of vegetables. Remove the 2 small packets of seasoning mix. Disregard directions for cooking vegetables on box. In a 2 cup measuring cup, dissolve contents of little white packets in a small amount of water. Mix well, then fill cup with 1 1/2 cups water. To this add 2 packets of stir fry seasoning mix and corn starch and set aside. Melt butter in Wok or hot skillet. Add shrimp and stir for 15 minutes. Add vegetables and stir for 3 minutes. Add seasoning mix. Stir until very bubbly. Serve over steaming hot rice.

WELSH
Theresa David
JEFFERSON DAVIS PARISH

Quick Chicken 'N Dumplings
SERVES 8

1 or 2 fryers
2 cans Butter-Me-Not biscuits
1 cup onions, chopped
1 cup bell pepper, chopped
1/2 cup celery, chopped
1 tbsp. parsley
3 pats of butter
1 tbsp. green onions
Salt and pepper to taste

Cut fryers in serving pieces. Heat large pot with 3 pats butter and place chicken pieces in pot. Simmer till they turn a light golden brown. Add vegetables, cooking only to saute'. Add boiling water (about 3/4 full) and cook for 1 hour. Add salt and pepper. Take 2 cans of biscuits, open and place each one on a large sheet of wax paper covered with plenty of flour. Roll each biscuit with rolling pin until very thin. Stack about 6 biscuits on top of each other and cut with a sharp knife into finger size strips (continue this procedure until both cans of biscuits are cut). Drop strips into boiling chicken broth. Cover and cook about 20 minutes.

WESTLAKE

Marguerite Oliver
CALCASIEU PARISH

Fish Etouffee (Sac-A-Lait)
SERVES 6-8

1 1/2 lbs. fresh fish fillets
1 can cream of mushroom soup
1 bell pepper, chopped
2 banana peppers, chopped
2 celery stalks, chopped
2 cloves garlic, chopped
Onion tops or parsley
1 block oleo or 1/2 cup butter
1 or 2 tbsp. paprika
Red pepper
Salt

Saute' onion, bell pepper, banana peppers, celery and garlic in block of butter until clear. Add can of mushroom soup. Stir well. Add paprika to get your reddish etouffee color. Let cook on low to medium heat for a few minutes. Season fish with salt and red pepper. Add fish to sauce and let cook for 20 to 30 minutes. DO NOT ADD water to fish and sauce. If you see that it is too thick, just before it is cooked you can add a little water. Just before cooking is done add onion tops or parsley or both. Serve over rice.

YOUNGSVILLE

Gail Hulin
LAFAYETTE PARISH

Central Section

Alexandria	Grand Coteau	Oakdale
Arnaudville	Hessmer	Oberlin
Basile	Hornbeck	Opelousas
Boyce	Kinder	Pine Prairie
Bunkie	Krotz Springs	Pineville
Chataignier	Lawtell	Pitkin
Cheneyville	Lecompte	Pollock
Colfax	Leesville	Port Barre
Cottonport	Leonville	Rosepine
DeRidder	Mamou	Simmesport
Dry Prong	Mansura	Simpson
Elizabeth	Marksville	Sunset
Eunice	Melville	Turkey Creek
Evergreen	Montgomery	Ville Platte
Georgetown	Moreauville	Washington
Glenmora		

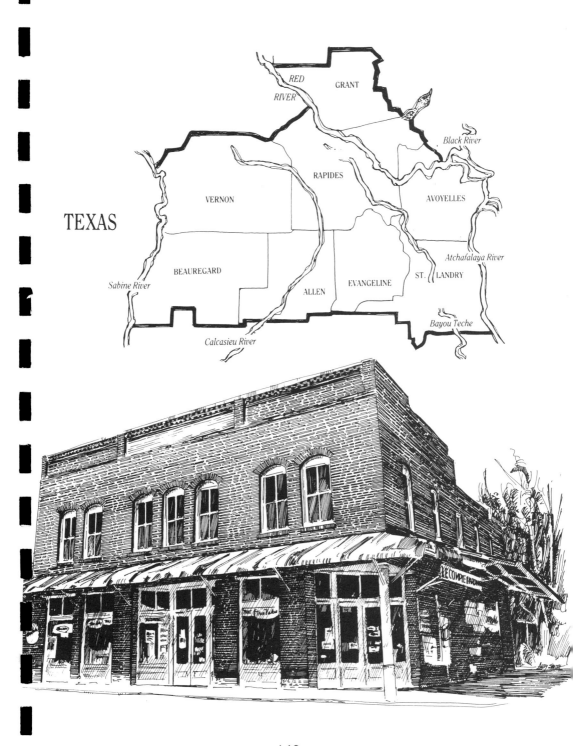

TEXAS

RED RIVER

GRANT

Black River

RAPIDES

VERNON

AVOYELLES

BEAUREGARD

Sabine River

ALLEN

EVANGELINE

ST. LANDRY

Atchafalaya River

Calcasieu River

Bayou Teche

Smoked Brisket
SERVES 15-20

10-13 lbs. brisket, pork or beef
20 lbs. Kingsford Mesquite Charcoal
Chips - Mesquite or Hickory or Pecan
Tony Chachere Creole Seasoning
Lea and Perrin or Liquid Hickory Smoke
Dark brown sugar
Lemon pepper

Trim fat off meat. Shake Tony's and lemon pepper on meat (you can use Accent to tenderize the meat if desired). Sprinkle liquid smoke over meat. Apply dark brown sugar on top of meat. Be sure the fat side is on the bottom and lean meat is on top. Let it set in refrigerator for 3 hours. Put it on smoker grill. Cooking time is 10 to 14 hours. This can be cooked in oven by wrapping meat in aluminum foil and cooked for 5 hours at 375 degrees.

ALEXANDRIA

Sam D. Morrison, Jr.
RAPIDES PARISH

Smothered Chicken And Gravy
SERVES 5

1 chicken
2 tsp. sugar
2 or 3 onions, sliced
1 tbsp. grease
Water
Black and red pepper
Garlic salt
Salt

First you burn your sugar in the hot grease. Put chicken in and brown it well. Then add seasonings and onions and a little water. Cook on medium heat till done. Keep adding water as needed to make gravy.

ARNAUDVILLE
Stan J. Wyble
ST. LANDRY PARISH

151

Louisiana Fig Cake

SERVES 12

1 quart canned figs
2 sticks oleo
1 cup pecans, chopped
2 eggs, beaten
2 cups flour
2 tsp. vanilla flavoring
2 tsp. baking soda
1/4 tsp. nutmeg
1/4 tsp. cinnamon

Pour figs into bowl, sprinkle soda over figs, let melt together.
Add egg, oleo, vanilla, cinnamon and nutmeg. Stir well. Add
flour and pecans. Stir until well mixed. Pour into well buttered
pan and bake 40 to 50 minutes at 350 degrees. Let cool for
15 minutes then cut into squares.

BASILE

Betty L. Aguillard
EVANGELINE PARISH

Stuffed Pistollette Rolls

SERVES 24

2 packages Pistollette Rolls
1 lb. ground meat
1 package frozen or fresh broccoli
3/4 lb. Velveeta cheese
1 medium onion, chopped
1/2 tsp. creole seasoning
Dash of garlic powder
Oleo

Cut at an angle the end of each roll. Cut out inside of roll, cut out bread in the top you cut off and save top. Saute' ground meat, onion, the creole seasoning and a dash of garlic powder. Cook until meat is done. Drain off all liquid. Cook broccoli until tender. Drain well. Add cheese, (can use hot Velveeta) stirring until cheese is melted. Add to meat mixture and mix well. With teaspoon fill each roll with mixture. Replace cap end. Dip in melted garlic butter completely covering roll. Bake at 350 degrees.

BOYCE

Jeanette Nichols
RAPIDES PARISH

Aunt Iris's Dressing Mix
SERVES 30

3 lbs. lean ground pork
1 lb. lean ground beef
3 cans cream of mushroom soup
2 large cans deviled ham
6 cups raw rice, cooked
Large pan of corn bread, crumbled
4 large onions, chopped

2 bell peppers, chopped
4 cloves garlic, chopped
2 ribs celery, chopped
Red pepper to taste
Small amount of salt
1 tbsp. Worcestershire sauce
Green onions, chopped
Chopped parsley to taste

Saute' meats lightly, enough to separate into small particles. Add onions, bell peppers, celery, garlic and Worcestershire. Cook, stirring often, about 10 minutes. Add water to cover ingredients. Bring to a boil, cover, lower to simmer and cook for 1 hour. Add deviled ham and cook 15 minutes. Add soup, cook 15 minutes stirring often as this has a tendency to stick. Add green onions and parsley. This freezes very well. To make dressing, cook rice and add mix, for dirty rice. Or when using corn bread for corn bread dressing moisten with chicken broth, and add mix. Makes a delicious corn bread dressing. Bon Appetit!!!

BUNKIE
Ina Claire Marchive
AVOYELLES PARISH

Chicken And Sausage Gumbo
SERVES 8

2 cups roux
1 fryer or hen
2 lbs. smoked sausage, sliced
1 onion, chopped
1/2 cup onion tops, chopped
Parsley
Salt, black and red pepper to taste

In a large pot put about 3 qts. of water. When hot add 2 cups of roux. Stir constantly until well dissolved. When boiling add cut fryer or cut hen. Also add sausage and chopped onions and about 1/2 cup chopped onion tops and parsley. Season to taste with seasonings. For fryer cook about one hour. If hen is used cook until meat is tender.

CHATAIGNIER

Bernice Lavergne
EVANGELINE PARISH

Pork Bones And Rice Jambalaya
SERVES 6-8

2 cups cooked rice
3 lbs. pork bones or pork steaks
3 tbsp. bacon drippings or shortening
1 can cream of mushroom soup
1/2 can water
3 tbsp. flour
1 medium onion, chopped

1/2 cup green onions, chopped
2 cloves garlic, minced
2 tbsp. parsley, minced (dried or fresh)
1/4 cup bell pepper, chopped (red or green)
1/2 cup celery, chopped
Salt and pepper to taste

Brown pork bones or pork steaks (cut into small pieces) in shortening or bacon drippings. Remove bones or steak from pot. Add flour to drippings and make a roux. Add vegetables to roux and cook until soft. Add cream of mushroom soup and water. Stir frequently to prevent sticking. Stir until well blended. Add cooked rice, a little at a time, until well blended. Add salt and pepper. You can add a little more water if necessary. Add bones or steak and mix well. Cook covered in 300 degree oven for 45 minutes or until bones or steak are well cooked. Can also be cooked on top of the stove over low heat. Uncover and cook a few minutes longer if the jambalaya is too moist. Serve with green salad and hot French bread.

CHENEYVILLE
Johnny Klock
RAPIDES PARISH

Pecan Pie
SERVES 8

3 eggs
1/2 cup sugar
1/4 tsp. salt
1 cup light corn syrup (Karo)
1/2 tsp. vanilla
2 cups pecans, broken
Whipped cream

Beat eggs slightly. Add other ingredients. Mix well. Line plate with plain pastry. Pour in filling and bake 45 minutes in slow oven at 300 degrees. May be garnished with whipped cream and pecans.

COLFAX
Mrs. Mandalou Bowen
GRANT PARISH

Sweet Potato Casserole
SERVES 6

3 medium sweet potatoes, peeled
1/2 cup pecans, chopped
1/2 cup bananas, mashed
1/8 cup softened margarine or butter
1/8 cup brown sugar, packed
1/2 tsp. cinnamon
1/8 tsp. salt
Marshmallows

Boil potatoes till tender. Mash potatoes and mix in all ingredients except marshmallows. Pour into a greased casserole and top with marshmallows. Cook at 350 degrees until marshmallows melt or brown.

COTTONPORT
Nita Poret Baudoin
AVOYELLES PARISH

"My Special" Lasagna
SERVES 12

1 lb. ground chuck
1 lb. can of stewed tomatoes
2 6 oz. cans tomato paste
1 10 oz. package of lasagna noodles
24 oz. creamstyle cottage cheese
2 eggs, beaten

1 lb. Mozzarella cheese, sliced
1/2 tsp. garlic powder
3 tbsp. parsley, chopped
2 1/2 tsp. salt
1/2 cup Parmesan cheese
1/2 tsp. black pepper

Brown meat slowly. Spoon off excess fat. Add garlic powder, 1 tbsp. parsley, 1 1/2 tsp. salt, tomatoes and tomato paste. Simmer covered until thick, about 15 minutes. Meanwhile cook noodles until tender, drain and rinse in cold water. Combine cottage cheese, eggs, 1 tsp. salt, pepper, 2 tbsp. parsley and Parmesan cheese. Grease 9" x 13" x 2" baking dish. Place half the noodles on bottom of dish, spread 1/2 of the cottage cheese mix. Add 1/2 Mozzarella cheese then 1/2 of the meat mixture. Repeat layers until you have 2 full layers of each mixture. Bake 30 minutes in 375 degree oven. Let stand 10 to 15 minutes before serving.

DERIDDER
Frances A. Jouban
BEAUREGARD PARISH

Squash Casserole
SERVES 10

2 lbs. squash, sliced
1 small onion, chopped
1 tbsp. oleo, melted
1 8 oz. sour cream
2 tbsp. pimento
1/2 cup oleo
1 10 3/4 oz. can cream of chicken soup, undiluted
1 8 oz. package herb-seasoned stuffing mix
Salt and pepper to taste

Cook squash and onion until tender and drain. Season with
salt, pepper and 1 tbsp. oleo. Stir in chicken soup, sour
cream and pimento. In separate bowl, combine 1/2 cup oleo
and stuffing mix. Stir until well-blended. Combine half of
stuffing mix and squash mixture. Spoon into 2 quart casserole
dish. Top with remaining stuffing mix. Bake 375 degrees for
30 minutes. Can be prepared ahead of time and frozen.

DRY PRONG
Ronda Shirley
GRANT PARISH

Chicken And Dumplings
SERVES 20

1 hen
4 or 5 cans biscuits
1 stick margarine
1 tbsp. garlic salt
1 tbsp. black pepper
Salt to taste

Cook chicken till it will come off bone. Take out bones and set aside to cool. Be sure you have enough broth to put your dough in after adding ingredients (if chicken is small, use only 4 cans of biscuits). Roll each biscuit and cut in small pieces and add to the broth 3 or 4 at a time. Add meat and cook for a few minutes on medium heat. Then cover and let stand for a while.

ELIZABETH

Virgie Mitchell
ALLEN PARISH

Rice Cooker Seafood Jambalaya
SERVES 4-6

1 lb. peeled shrimp
1 pint oysters
1 can crabmeat
1 4 oz. can mushroom pieces
1 can beef broth
1 1/2 cup raw rice
1 medium onion, chopped
1 medium bell pepper, chopped
1 stick oleo, softened
Salt and pepper to taste

Add all ingredients into rice cooker, mix well, turn it on. Takes approximately 30 minutes. 2 lbs. peeled crawfish tails may be used instead of the shrimp, oysters, and crabmeat. Smoked sausage (cut into pieces) may also be used to make sausage jambalaya.

EUNICE
Elaine Oge'
ST. LANDRY PARISH

Never Fail Pie Crust
MAKES 5 CRUSTS

4 cups all purpose flour
1 tsp. baking powder
1/2 tsp. salt
1 tbsp. sugar
1 3/4 cups shortening
1 egg, beaten
1 tbsp. vinegar
1/2 cup cold water

Combine dry ingredients; cut in shortening until mixture resembles coarse meal. Stir in remaining ingredients. Divide dough into 5 equal parts; shape each into a ball and wrap tightly. Chill. May be stored up to 2 weeks in refrigerator. Yield: Pastry for five 9 inch pies. If desired, you may use the pastry immediately after mixing. Especially good for fruit or pecan pies.

EVERGREEN
Carol Heiman Miller
AVOYELLES PARISH

Chicken Broccoli Casserole
SERVES 6

2 10 oz. packages frozen broccoli, cooked
2 cups chicken breasts, cooked and chopped
2 cans cream of chicken soup
1 cup mayonnaise
1/2 cup sharp cheddar cheese, grated
1/2 cup bread crumbs
1 1/2 tsp. lemon juice
3/4 tsp. curry powder
1 tbsp. melted butter

Place cooked broccoli in rectangular casserole dish. Cover with cooked, chopped chicken. Combine soup, mayonnaise, lemon juice and curry powder. Mix and pour over chicken. Cover with grated cheese and bread crumbs. Top with melted butter. Bake at 325 degrees for about 30 minutes.

GEORGETOWN
Bettye Lincecum Elliott
GRANT PARISH

Kevin's "Special" Stuffed Bell Peppers

SERVES 8

1 lb. ground meat
8 large bell peppers
1/2 cup bell pepper, chopped
1 large onion, chopped
1/2 cup celery, diced
1 box Uncle Ben's Wild Rice/Mushroom
1 8 oz. can tomato sauce
2/3 cup soda cracker crumbs
6 strips bacon
1 1/2 cup Velveeta cheese, grated
1/8 tsp. garlic salt
1/4 tsp. salt
1/8 tsp. black pepper

Cut top of bell peppers off and remove seeds. Put peppers in large covered stew pan with 1 inch water in bottom. Steam at low heat until they turn bright green in color, about 20 minutes. Remove, cool and peel. In large skillet brown the ground beef, bell pepper, celery, onion and seasoning. Cook rice according to box instructions. Fry bacon crisp and crumble in small bowl. Stuff each pepper and place in baking dish. Add 3/4 cup water to tomato sauce and pour over peppers, allowing about 1/2 inch juice in bottom of pan. Sprinkle cheese and bacon crumbles on top. Bake 350 degrees for 30 to 40 minutes. Serve hot.

GLENMORA

Jeri Mizell
RAPIDES PARISH

Plantation Sweet Potato Pones
SERVES 8

4 large sweet potatoes (raw)
2 eggs
1 cup milk
1/2 cup brown sugar
1/2 cup molasses
1/2 cup butter
1/2 tsp. nutmeg
1/2 tsp. cinnamon
1/2 tsp. ground cloves
1 lemon rind, grated
1/2 orange rind, grated

Grate raw potatoes, lemon and orange peels. Beat eggs and sugar. Add potatoes, spices, molasses, milk and butter. Pour into a greased baking dish. Bake for 1 hour in 325-350 degree oven. Serve hot with meat or chicken. Can be cut and is good cold.

GRAND COTEAU

Amy Lowery
ST. LANDRY PARISH

Crawfish Dip
SERVES 8-10

1 lb. crawfish tails
1/2 bunch green onions, chopped
1 stick margarine
Parsley
2 tbsp. flour
1 can mushrooms, (bits and stems)
1 1/2 cartons sour cream
Salt and pepper
Hot sauce if desired

Saute' 1/2 bunch of green onions, 1 stick of margarine and 1 lb. of crawfish tails until done. Add parsley and 2 tbsp. of flour to thicken. Add 1 can of bits and stems mushrooms and 1 1/2 cartons of sour cream. Salt and pepper to taste. Cook slowly, then serve warm with chips.

HESSMER
Fay D. Guillory
AVOYELLES PARISH

Beans And Sausage
SERVES 8-10

1 lb. ground beef
1 lb. link sausage
1 small onion, chopped
1 can pork n' beans
1 can jalapeno pinto beans
1 can chili beans
1 can tomato sauce
1 can water
Tony's Creole Seasonings
Salt
Pepper

Brown hamburger or ground beef with onions. Drain off
excess oil. In slow cooker combine beef, onions, sausage
(cut in small pieces), can of pork n' beans, can of jalapeno
pinto beans, can of chili beans, can of tomato sauce and can
of water. Season to taste and cook for 1 to 1 1/2 hour. Serve
over rice.

HORNBECK
Betty Green
VERNON PARISH

Crawfish And Rice Casserole
SERVES 8-10

1 medium onion, chopped
3 stalks celery, chopped
3 small bell pepper, chopped
2 lbs. cleaned crawfish
1 stick butter or oleo
1 can golden mushroom soup
1 lb. sharp cheddar cheese, grated
2 cups rice, cooked
1 tsp. concentrated liquid crab and shrimp boil
Salt and pepper to taste

Saute' vegetables in butter. Salt and pepper crawfish to taste.
Add crawfish to vegetables and cook for 15 minutes. Add crab
and shrimp boil and stir well. Add soup, cover and simmer for
5 minutes. Layer in a casserole dish; 1 layer of cooked rice, 1
layer of crawfish mixture and 1 layer of grated cheese.
Repeat layers. Bake at 350 degrees for 20 minutes.

KINDER
Myra Benoit
ALLEN PARISH

Yam Nut Cake

SERVES 30

2 cups oil
3 cups cooked sweet potatoes
1 1/2 cup milk
6 cups sugar
1 can condensed milk
9 eggs
8 cups flour
2 cups chopped nuts
2 tsp. salt
2 tsp. soda
1 tsp. cinnamon
2 tsp. vanilla

Cream oil and sugar. Add eggs one at a time. Add mashed sweet potatoes. Mix together flour, salt, soda and cinnamon and add to above mixture. Add milks and vanilla and beat well. Add chopped nuts and mix. Bake at 350 degrees in greased 9" X 13" pan until done. About 1 hour. Makes about 60 squares.

KROTZ SPRINGS

Susie Bergeron
ST. LANDRY PARISH

Geneva's Easy Potato Casserole
SERVES 6-8

4 cups instant potatoes
4 cups water
2 cups cold milk
1 stick margarine
3 tbsp. bacon bits
1 can cream of mushroom soup
1 cup cheese, grated
1 tsp. salt
1/2 tsp. cayenne pepper
1 tsp. Accent'
1 medium onion, chopped
1 medium bell pepper, chopped

In a large pot, bring to a boil all ingredients except instant potatoes, milk and cheese. Let simmer for 15 minutes. Remove from heat. Add instant potatoes and milk, mixing well. Pour into a large casserole dish or baking pan. Top with grated cheese. Bake at 300 degrees for 15 minutes. NOTE: Can be placed in microwave instead of oven if in microwave safe casserole dish. Microwave on high for 6 minutes.

LAWTELL
Geneva D. Prudhomme
ST. LANDRY PARISH

Crawfish Linguine
SERVES 4-6

1 lb. peeled cooked crawfish
1 12 oz. package of linguine or spaghetti
1/4 cup parsley, chopped
1/4 cup celery, chopped
1 lb. mushrooms, sliced
1/4 tsp. red pepper
1/2 tsp. salt
1/2 cup or 1 stick unsalted butter
2 cloves garlic, chopped
2 tbsp. olive oil
1/2 cup white wine
1/2 cup Parmesan cheese
Louisiana hot sauce to taste

Cook pasta according to package while preparing crawfish sauce. In large skillet (do not use iron skillet), melt butter with olive oil, add onion, parsley, celery, garlic and saute'. Add mushrooms and cook 3 minutes. Add white wine and bring to a boil. Add crawfish, red pepper, hot sauce and salt. Cook 5 to 8 minutes. In a large pot, pour crawfish mixture in with drained linguine, toss with grated Parmesan.

LECOMPTE
Colleen Poole Hursey
RAPIDES PARISH

Chicken And Dumplings
SERVES 8

1 chicken
6 tbsp. shortening
3 cups all purpose flour
4 tsp. baking powder
1 1/2 cup milk
Tony's Creole Seasoning
Pepper
2 tsp. salt

Boil chicken in a large pot until done. Remove chicken from broth and set aside. Cool slightly and debone. While chicken is cooling, cut shortening into flour, baking powder and salt until mixture resembles crumbs. Stir in milk. Knead lightly. Roll out on cutting board until thin. Cut dumplings in about 1 inch strips. Drop one by one into boiling chicken broth. Then put deboned chicken back in pot. Season to taste with salt, pepper, and Tony's Creole Seasoning. Cook uncovered 15 minutes. Cover and cook about 20 minutes longer on low heat.

LEESVILLE
Jewel Strickland
VERNON PARISH

Eggplant Casserole
SERVES 6

1 large eggplant
3/4 lb. ground beef
3/4 lb. ground pork
1/2 cup cheese, grated
1 egg
1 can cream of mushroom soup
1 cup bread crumbs
1/2 cup bell pepper, chopped
1/2 cup onion, chopped
1/2 cup celery, chopped
Salt and pepper to taste

Peel eggplant, chop and boil in small amount of water until tender. Cook meat; add onion, bell pepper and celery. Add eggplant. Cook for about 10 minutes. Add cheese and soup and cook until cheese is melted. Add beaten egg and 1/2 cup of bread crumbs. Mix well. Pour into casserole dish. Sprinkle with remaining bread crumbs. Dot with butter and bake for about 20 to 25 minutes at 375 degrees.

LEONVILLE

Melissa Robin
ST. LANDRY PARISH

Catfish Courtbouillon
SERVES SEVERAL

Fresh catfish, cut in chunks	1 tbsp. oil
1 very large yellow onion, chopped	1 can water
1 cup onion tops, chopped	Garlic powder
1/2 cup parsley, chopped	Cloves
1 can tomato sauce	Red and black pepper
1 tbsp. flour	Salt

Put a little oil, about 1 tbsp. in thick pot. Put in pieces of catfish cut in chunks. Season with salt, black and red pepper, garlic powder, salt or cloves. Add onion and onion tops and chopped parsley. Pour in 1 can of tomato sauce, sprinkle flour then fill empty can of tomato sauce with water and pour over everything in pot. Mix thoroughly with hands, making sure all is mixed well. Put on high flame. Lower flame as soon as fish begins to cook. Cook in covered pot on low (medium flame). Stir every once in a while by picking pot up and shaking pot around. Do not stir in pot with spoon. This will keep sauce from sticking. Dish is cooked as soon as the onions are cooked (Do not cook until fish breaks up). About 30 minutes (depends on amount of fish)

MAMOU
Rita A.V. Pierrottie
EVANGELINE PARISH

Chocolate Cake Pudding

SERVES 8

1 cup flour
1/4 tsp. salt
3/4 cup sugar
2 tsp. baking powder
1 1/2 tbsp. cocoa
1/2 cup milk
2 tbsp. melted butter
1 tsp. vanilla
1/2 cup pecans, chopped
3/4 cup sugar
3 tbsp. cocoa
1 cup water

Sift together flour, salt, sugar, baking powder and cocoa. Stir in milk, butter, vanilla and pecans. Pour into a 9" baking pan. Mix 3/4 cup sugar with 3 tbsp. cocoa and sprinkle evenly over cake batter. Pour water on top of sugar mixture. Do not stir. Bake at 325 degrees for 40 to 45 minutes or until cake part is done. Serve warm.

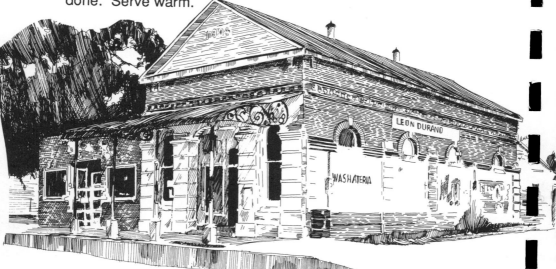

MANSURA

Debra Bernard
AVOYELLES PARISH

Cornish Hen Jambalaya
SERVES 4

2 Cornish game hens, halved
Oil for browning
1 large onion, chopped
1/2 large bell pepper, chopped
3 cloves fresh garlic, chopped
1 fresh tomato, chopped
2 tsp. Worcestershire
1/4 cup wine (red or white)
2 cups rice
All purpose Cajun seasoning
Water

Season hen halves with Cajun seasoning. Brown hen halves
in oil and remove. Saute' onion, bell pepper, garlic and
tomato until wilted. Add 1/2 cups water, Worcestershire sauce
and wine. Return hens to mixture, cover and simmer until
tender (about 1 hour). Remove hen halves and measure
liquid. Add rice and enough water to total 4 cups liquid. Bring
to a boil, lower heat and simmer until rice is cooked. Return
hen halves to top of rice and place under the broiler to brown.
(Amount of liquid needed will vary with kind of pot and
temperature adjustments.)

MARKSVILLE
Mrs. Steven V. Dauzat
AVOYELLES PARISH

177

Murl's Corn Bread Dressing
SERVES 16

Baked corn bread
2 lbs. ground beef
1 envelope Lipton Onion Soup
2 cans mushroom soup
1 can chicken broth
1/2 cup green onion tops, chopped
1 cup water
Salt and pepper to taste

Brown ground beef. Drain off grease. Add envelope of onion soup mix, 2 cans mushroom soup, 1 can chicken broth and 1 cup of water. Simmer this for about 25 to 30 minutes. Mix meat mixture with crumbled corn bread. Put into 9" X 13" baking dish in the oven for about 20 minutes at 350 degrees. If more liquid is needed, add more chicken broth.

MELVILLE
Murline J. Murray
ST. LANDRY PARISH

Jack's Favorite Shrimp Creole
SERVES 6

1/2 cup margarine
1 large onion, chopped
2 bell peppers, chopped
4 ribs celery, chopped
2 tbsp. flour
2 small cans tomato sauce
3 cans stewed tomatoes
2 lbs. peeled shrimp
1 can Rotel tomatoes
Cooked rice
1/4 tsp. red pepper
Salt and pepper to taste

Melt margarine and cook onions, celery and bell pepper until tender. Stir in flour. Add tomato sauce and canned tomatoes. Cook for 20 minutes. Add shrimp and cook for 10 minutes. Salt and pepper to taste. Serve over hot steamed rice.

MONTGOMERY
Darrell Granger
GRANT PARISH

Tilly's Hot Rolls
SERVES 24

2 cups very warm water
2 packages dry yeast
7 tbsp. sugar
1 tbsp. salt
1/4 cup Crisco shortening
5 1/4 cups all purpose flour

Combine water and 2 tbsp. sugar, stir twice, add yeast and allow to stand until it floats. Add salt, Crisco shortening and remaining sugar. Add flour, mix well and stir for 10 minutes. Place in greased bowl, oil top lightly and allow to rise until doubled. Punch down. Roll on floured board. Shape into rolls, place in greased pan and oil top very lightly. Let rise until doubled. Bake at 400 degrees until browned. Remove from oven and butter top.

MOREAUVILLE
Mathilda Mayeux
AVOYELLES PARISH

Syrian-Lebanese Salad
SERVES 7-10

1 large head of iceberg lettuce
3 tomatoes
1 cucumber
1/2 cup good quality olive oil
2 or 3 pods garlic crushed with a little salt
2 or 3 mint leaves, crushed (if desired)
1 large lemon, squeezed
Salt and pepper to taste

Break lettuce and dry very thoroughly. Dice tomatoes and cucumber. Add mint leaves if used. Add garlic, olive oil and lemon juice. Mix very thoroughly - tasting as you mix. You may need to add more salt or red pepper.

OAKDALE
Mrs. George B. Mowad
ALLEN PARISH

White Lima Beans And Sausage
SERVES 6

2 cups dried baby lima beans
2 quarts water
2 tbsp. bacon drippings
1 lb. sausage
Salt and pepper to taste

Combine first five ingredients and boil over medium heat for three hours. After three hours, cut sausage into 2 inch pieces and add to bean mixture. Cook an additional thirty minutes. Serve with cooked rice or corn bread.

OBERLIN
Emily Adams
ALLEN PARISH

Cajun Ribs
SERVES 4-6

4 lbs. lean pork ribs
9 oz. strained peaches
1/3 cup catsup
1/3 cup vinegar
1/2 cup brown sugar
1 clove garlic
2 tbsp. soy sauce
2 tsp. ginger
2 tbsp. Worcestershire sauce
1 tsp. salt
2 tsp. hot sauce

Brown ribs "quickly" in "hot" oil. Mix remaining ingredients.
Put ribs into baking dish. Pour sauce over them. Bake at 350
degrees for 1 hour or until done. Can be cooked on grill. Use
sauce for basting. For spicier sauce add 1 tsp. red pepper.

OPELOUSAS
Ruby A. Johnson
ST. LANDRY PARISH

Broccoli Corn Bread
SERVES 6-8

2 boxes Jiffy Corn Bread Mix
1 1/3 cup cottage cheese
1 medium onion, chopped
4 eggs
1 1/2 stick of margarine, melted
1 box frozen chopped broccoli, thawed
1 or 2 jalapeno peppers, chopped (optional)
1/2 tsp. salt
Red pepper, dash

Mix well, folding in the broccoli last. Put into 9" X 13" X
2" pan. Bake at 350 degrees for 45 minutes. (Use non-stick
spray on Pan)

PINE PRAIRIE
Brandy Dupre'
EVANGELINE PARISH

Mom's Old Fashioned Scalded Corn Bread SERVES 8

2/3 cup self rising flour
1 3/4 cup corn meal
1 tsp. salt
1/2 tsp. soda
2 tsp. sugar
1/4 cup oil

2 1/2 tsp. baking powder
Boiling water
1 beaten egg
3/4 cup buttermilk
1/4 cup milk

In large bowl stir up dry ingredients. Pour 1/4 cup oil in center. Then add enough boiling water stirring constantly, until all dry ingredients are just wet. Mixture will be thick and gummy. Add 1 beaten egg and buttermilk and milk. Stir and mix well (mixture will be the consistency of cake batter). Heat black skillet with 3 tbsp. oil. Pour batter into a very hot skillet so that mixture will fry when poured in. Dip some of the oil over top of bread. Bake 450 degrees for about 45 minutes or until browned. (If not browned on top turn on broiler a few minutes to brown good). Turn up on plate and slice and let cool a few minutes. Yum Yum - then get the mustard greens ready!

PINEVILLE
Lisa LaCour
RAPIDES PARISH

Steamed Shrimp
SERVES 2-3

3 lbs. large shrimp in shells
2 large onions, chopped fine
3 ribs celery, chopped fine
1 bell pepper, chopped fine
2/3 cup oil or butter
Garlic powder to taste
Black and red pepper to taste
Salt

Dehead shrimp. Season Shrimp in shell with salt, black pepper, red pepper and garlic powder. Put shrimp in hot oil and stir until shrimp turns pink. Add onions, celery and bell pepper. Mix well and cook for 15 minutes. When done, use a slotted spoon to move shrimp to platter. Serve juice in small bowls. When eating, suck on shrimp first, then peel shrimp. Shrimp can be dipped in juice or dip juice with French bread. Serve with green salad. Delicious!

PITKIN
Mattie Rose Rivers
VERNON PARISH

Chicken Spaghetti
SERVES 10

5 cups cooked chicken
1 can chicken broth
1 lb. cheddar cheese
1 4 oz. jar pimento
2 cans mushroom soup
1 8 oz. package spaghetti
Salt and pepper to taste

Cook spaghetti according to package directions. Drain and
combine all ingredients, except cheese. Put in casserole dish
and top with cheese. Heat in a 350 degree oven until
hot and bubbly.

POLLOCK
Betty Roshto
GRANT PARISH

Peppered Steak
SERVES 6-8

1 round steak (2-2 1/2 lbs.)
2 medium onions, chopped
1 medium bell pepper, chopped
1 large bell pepper, cut in rings
1 16 oz. can stewed tomatoes
1 clove garlic, chopped
1/4 cup vegetable oil
water
Salt and cayenne pepper to taste

Cut round steak into 2" or 3" serving size pieces. Season with salt and cayenne pepper. Brown meat in oil in heavy dutch oven. After meat is brown, drain most of oil, add chopped onions, bell pepper, and garlic. Cook until onions are wilted. Add stewed tomatoes and water. Cover, stir and add water when necessary. Cook until tender. Add rings of bell pepper on top of meat, cover and simmer for 20 minutes. Serve over cooked rice.

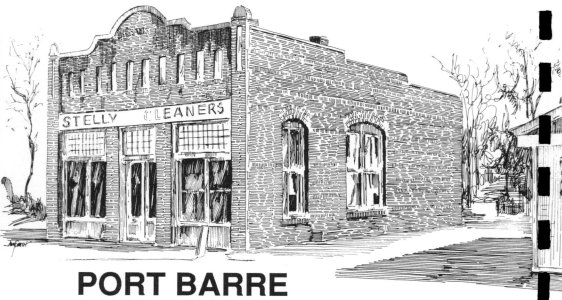

PORT BARRE
Audrey C. Thibodeaux
ST. LANDRY PARISH

Seven Layer Salad
SERVES 8-10

1/2 head of lettuce broken into bite sizes
3/4 cup green onions, chopped
3/4 cup bell pepper, chopped
1 cup carrots, shredded
3/4 cup celery, chopped
1 8 oz. package frozen green peas
1 10 oz. cheddar cheese, shredded
2 tsp. sugar
1 1/2 cup mayonnaise
1 3.25 oz. jar Bac'n Pieces

Layer first five ingredients. Cook green peas in just enough water to cover for 5 minutes. Drain. Layer peas over vegetables. Sprinkle sugar over peas. Spread mayonnaise over peas. Add cheese and Bac'n Pieces in order. Cover and refrigerate over night.

ROSEPINE
Elaine Fontenot
VERNON PARISH

Crawfish Fettucine

SERVES 6-8

1 1/2 sticks butter
1 1/2 onions, chopped
1 bell pepper, chopped
2 ribs celery, chopped
2 tbsp. flour
1 lb. crawfish tails
1/2 lb. Velveeta cheese, cubed
1 pint Half 'n Half cream

Parmesan cheese
1 clove garlic, minced
1/2 package fettucine noodles
Salt and pepper
1 tbsp. pimento
1 tbsp. jalapeno peppers

Saute' first 4 ingredients for 15 minutes. Add flour. Cover and cook on low fire for 15 minutes (stirring frequently). Add crawfish tails. Stir well. Cover and cook for 20 minutes (stir often). Add cheese, cream, garlic, jalapeno, salt and pepper. Cover and cook for 20 minutes. Meanwhile boil noodles, drain and pour into sauce. Gently blend together, then pour into buttered dish and sprinkle on Parmesan cheese. Bake at 350 degrees for 15 to 20 minutes.

SIMMESPORT
Merion R. Rabalais
AVOYELLES PARISH

Onion Cheese Chicken Bake
SERVES 6

6 chicken breasts
4 tbsp. butter
1 small jar mushrooms, drained
1 can French fried onion rings
1 cup Swiss cheese, grated
1 tsp. seasoned salt
1 tsp. pepper

Skin and debone chicken breasts. Melt butter. Add seasonings. Roll chicken to coat. Bake 20 minutes at 400 degrees. Add mushrooms and bake 15 minutes. Sprinkle with onion rings, then cheese (I use a combination of cheeses). Cook about 5 minutes or until cheese bubbles.

SIMPSON
Bobbye L. Gordy
VERNON PARISH

Chocolate Peanut Butter Fudge
SERVES 8-10

4 level tbsp. cocoa
4 cups sugar
1 cup chopped nuts
2 cups milk
6 tbsp. peanut butter
1 tsp. vanilla
Dash of salt

Butter sides of heavy 2 quart saucepan. Sift sugar, cocoa and salt into saucepan. Add milk. Cook on medium heat, stirring frequently, until mixture boils. Keep boiling on low heat to soft ball stage on candy thermometer. Turn off heat, add peanut butter, vanilla and nuts. Stir and let stand for 15 minutes, beat until hardened a little. Pour into buttered pan. Allow to cool. Cut into squares.

SUNSET
Mrs. Carmen B. Daigle
ST. LANDRY PARISH

Sweet and Sour Meatballs
SERVES 10

1 to 2 cups bread crumbs
1 egg
1 medium onion, chopped
1 1/2 lb. ground meat
1 tsp. garlic powder
SAUCE:
Sweet and Sour sauce
Small bottle of Heinz Bar B Que Sauce

Make small balls and bake at 350 degrees until brown about
20 minutes. Combine sauces and pour over meat and simmer
for about 30 minutes.

TURKEY CREEK
Connie Chapelle
EVANGELINE PARISH

Crawfish Casserole

SERVES 4-6

3 cups cooked rice
1 cup onions, chopped
1 cup bell pepper, chopped
1 10 oz. box broccoli, thawed and chopped
1 can cream of mushroom soup
1 1/4 cup of milk
8 oz. jar of jalapeno Cheese Whiz
2 tbsp. butter
1 lb. crawfish
Salt and pepper

Saute' chopped onions and bell pepper in butter until clear
and tender. Add broccoli and cook until tender. Add all other
ingredients (except cooked rice). Cook 15 to 20 minutes on
medium heat. When crawfish are cooked, add cooked rice
and mix well.

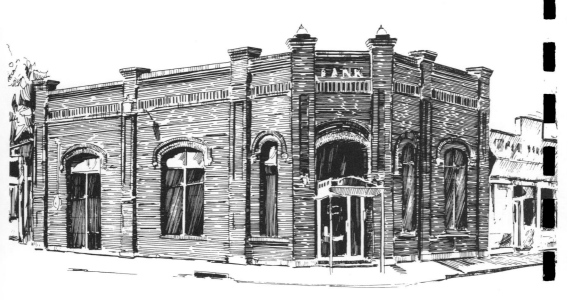

VILLE PLATTE
Helen Dardeau
EVANGELINE PARISH

Chicken Fricassee
SERVES 6

1 chicken, cut up
3 cups water
1 large onion, chopped
1 large bell pepper, chopped
3 tbsp. roux
Salt to taste
Cayenne pepper to taste

Boil water, roux, onion and bell pepper on medium fire until roux is dissolved. Add chicken and cook for 45 minutes. Serve over rice.

WASHINGTON
Darlene Lalonde
ST. LANDRY PARISH

195

Northwest Section

Arcadia
Ashland
Athens
Atlanta
Benton
Bossier City
Calvin
Campti
Chatham
Choudrant
Clarence
Cloutierville
Cotton Valley
Coushatta
Cullen
Doyline
Dubach
Gibsland

Gilliam
Grand Cane
Greenwood
Haughton
Haynesville
Hodge
Homer
Hosston
Jonesboro
Keatchie
Mansfield
Many
Minden
Mooringsport
Mount Lebanon
Natchez
Natchitoches
Oil City

Plain Dealing
Pleasant Hill
Provencal
Ringgold
Robeline
Rodessa
Ruston
Saline
Sarepta
Shongaloo
Shreveport
Simsboro
Springhill
Vienna
Vivian
Winnfield
Zwolle

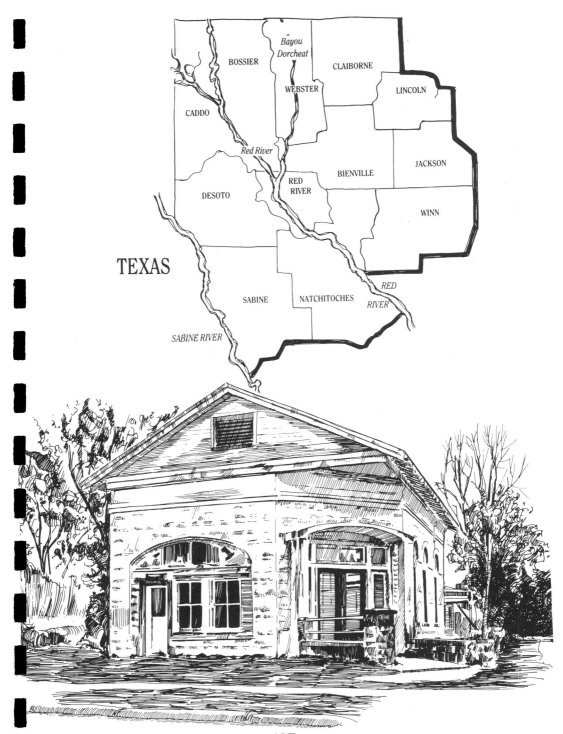

TEXAS

BOSSIER

Bayou Dorcheat

CLAIBORNE

WEBSTER

LINCOLN

CADDO

Red River

BIENVILLE

JACKSON

DESOTO

RED RIVER

WINN

SABINE

NATCHITOCHES

RED RIVER

SABINE RIVER

Sherried Shrimp

SERVES 6-8

1 pint shrimp, cooked and deveined
6 tbsp. butter
3 tsp. flour
1 tsp. lemon juice
1 pint cream
1/2 pint sour cream
3 egg yolks
1/2 cup sherry or white wine
Salt
White pepper

Clean shrimp and cook 3 minutes in 3 tbsp. butter. Add lemon juice (I like more lemon so I use 1/2 cup). Cook 1 minute. Add 3 tbsp. butter, flour, eggs and cream which have been mixed together well. When thoroughly mixed add the sherry or white wine. Heat it thoroughly until it has thickened to the consistency of white sauce. Serve over long grain and wild rice. This is excellent as a side dish served with sliced turkey. It is also a wonderful luncheon main course. I have had it in my recipe file for nearly fifty years. Everyone always raves about the dish.

ARCADIA

Margaret Ramsey "Margo" Wilder
BIENVILLE PARISH

Chocolate Pie
SERVES 6-8

6 tbsp. plain flour
1 1/2 cups sugar
3 egg yolks
3 egg whites
3 tbsp. cocoa
1 large can of evaporated milk
1 baked pastry shell
1 tsp. vanilla
3 tbsp. butter or oleo
6 tbsp. sugar
Pinch of baking powder or cream of tartar

Mix flour, sugar and cocoa together and sift. Add beaten egg yolks. Add evaporated milk. Add flavoring and butter. Cook in double boiler until thick, stirring often (it takes this pie a little longer to thicken than usual but it is worth the waiting). Pour into baked pie shell. For meringue: beat egg whites, add pinch of baking powder or cream of tartar and continue beating until stiff. Add sugar and spread on pie and bake at 350 degrees until brown.

ASHLAND

Clovis H. Pullig
NATCHITOCHES PARISH

Buttermilk Biscuits
SERVES 8-10

2 cups self rising flour
1 tsp. sugar
1/4 tsp. soda
1/3 cup Crisco shortening
1 cup buttermilk
Butter, melted

Preheat oven to 425 degrees. Sift together flour, sugar and soda with pastry blender or two knives. Cut shortening into flour mixture until mixture resembles coarse crumbs. Stir in buttermilk. Knead dough on floured board or cloth 10 times or until smooth. Roll to 1/2 inch thickness and cut with round floured biscuit cutter. Place on ungreased baking sheet and bake for 12 to 15 minutes or until golden. Brush with melted butter. (NOTE: All purpose flour sift 1 tsp. baking powder and 1/2 tsp. salt with dry ingredients.)

ATHENS

Patricia A. Keene
CLAIBORNE PARISH

Chicken N' Dumplings
SERVES 6

1 fryer
1/2 cup green onions, chopped
1/2 cup celery, chopped
2 cups plain flour
1 can cream of chicken soup
2 tbsp. oil
1/2 cup milk
1/2 tsp. salt
Salt
Pepper
Thyme

Cook, debone chicken, add onions, celery, other seasonings and soup. Make dumpling, roll out and cut in strips. Add and cook until done. Very easy and very delicious.

ATLANTA
Iver S. McManus
WINN PARISH

Corn Casserole

SERVES 6-8

2 cans cream style corn
1 onion, chopped
1 stick margarine
1 package jalapeno corn bread mix
1 cup cheese, grated
1 egg

Saute' onion in margarine. Stir in corn, egg, cheese and corn bread mix. Bake at 325 degrees for 45 minutes. This is very easy to prepare and good for a church supper.

BENTON

Marilyn McGowen
BOSSIER PARISH

Okra And Tomatoes

SERVES 6-8

1 20 oz. can tomatoes
2 small packages of frozen okra
3 large stalks of celery, chopped coarsely
1 large yellow onion, chopped coarsely
Bacon grease or cooking oil
Salt
Garlic
Red Peppers, crushed

Take enough bacon grease or oil (bacon grease tastes better
-cooking oil is better for you) to saute' onions and celery. Heat
over hot burner until grease sizzles. Put in onion and celery
stirring constantly until onions start to melt. Add can of tomatoes and bring to a boil. Add okra and bring back to a boil (if
you use fresh okra you will need 2-20 oz. cans full). Add 1
tsp. garlic, salt and hot peppers to taste. Turn heat down to
low and cook slowly covered about 30 to 45 minutes. Great
as leftovers.

BOSSIER CITY

Jeannie Oates
BOSSIER PARISH

Red Beans with Rice

SERVES 8-10

1 lb. dried pinto beans	1/2 tsp. soda
1 1/2 lb. lean hamburger	Mexene Chili Powder
1 large onion, chopped	1/2 tsp. garlic powder
1 lb. smoked sausage	1/2 tsp. black pepper
Lean ham	1/2 tsp. red pepper (optional)
to season pinto beans	Salt to taste

Soak pinto beans overnight in cold water. Drain. Place beans in large boiler and cover with water. Add 1/2 tsp. soda. Bring to a boil; lower heat and simmer for a few minutes. Drain liquid. Cover beans with hot water and add ham and salt to taste. Cook until tender. Saute' hamburger, onion, garlic, black and red pepper and salt to taste. Add 4 to 5 tbsp. chili powder (more if desired). Saute' until done. Add to beans and cook slowly for about 45 minutes to 1 hour. Slice sausage into 1/2 inch slices. Add to beans and cook until done. Serve over rice.

CALVIN

Addie Mae Hodges
WINN PARISH

Jalapeno Corn Bread

SERVES 8-10

1/4 cup cooking oil	2 eggs
1 1/2 lbs. ground meat	1 cup milk
2/3 cup onion, chopped	1/2 cup Jalapenos, sliced
1/2 cup celery, chopped	1 tsp. salt
1 can cream-style corn	3/4 tsp. soda
(No. 2 size)	1 cup meal

Place oil in a baking dish measuring approximately 7" x 11" in pre-heated oven of 350 degrees. Saute' ground meat, onion and celery. Add seasonings, corn and jalapeno slices (I use canned slices; e.g. those used on Nachos) and set aside. Mix meal, eggs and milk. (this mixture should be real thin). Combine entire recipe and pour into heated oiled dish. Bake in center of oven 45 to 50 minutes until golden brown. Do not overcook.

CAMPTI

Ethel Mae Vercher
NATCHITOCHES PARISH

Chocolate Eclair Cake

SERVES 12

1 lb. Graham Crackers
2 boxes French vanilla instant pudding
1 9 oz. Cool Whip
3 1/2 cups milk
FROSTING:
2 packages Redi blend liquid or 1/2 cup cocoa
2 tsp. white Karo
2 tsp. vanilla
3 tbsp. softened margarine
3 tbsp. milk
1 1/2 cups powdered sugar

Butter bottom of 9" x 13" pan. Then line with whole Graham Crackers. Mix milk and pudding at medium speed for 2 minutes and fold in cool whip. Pour 1/2 mixture over Graham Crackers. Then put another layer of crackers and pour remaining pudding mixture on crackers and put another layer of crackers. Refrigerate 2 hours. Mix all ingredients for frosting together and mix well. Spread over crackers. Refrigerate 24 hours.

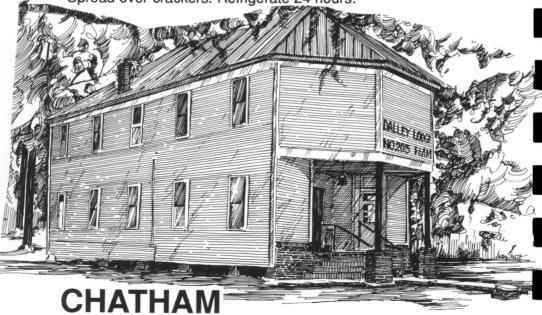

CHATHAM
Lynette Roberts
JACKSON PARISH

Melody Hills Ranch Smothered Venison
SERVES 2-4 PER POUND

Venison tenderloin or venison
steaks
1/2 cup white vinegar
1/2 cup water
Flour
Butter or margarine
Pam spray
Lemon pepper
Salt

Set oven at 350 degrees. Marinate or thaw venison in bowl or
pan of vinegar-water (1/2-1/2). Spread thawed, tender venison on cutting board and trim all fat. Rinse in cold water and
pat dry with paper towels. Spray skillet with Pam. Sprinkle
both sides of meat with lemon pepper and salt. Dust with
flour. Place piece by piece in skillet and brown on both sides
adding small amount of margarine. Spray Pam on long pan
(Pyrex or Corning Ware). Add meat. Cook for 1 hour. Cover
with foil for first 30 minutes, then remove foil for last 30 minutes. Test with fork for doneness. Will be brown on top.

CHOUDRANT
Mr. and Mrs James M. Ball
LINCOLN PARISH

Anymeal Skillet Potatoes

SERVES 3-4

4 medium white potaotes
1/2 cup green onions, chopped
1/2 cup white onions, chopped
1/2 cup celery, chopped
3 wieners, cut up
3 to 4 tbsp. cooking oil
Nature's seasonings to taste
1 tbsp. paprika

Wash and peel potatoes. Cut into cubes and put into skillet with 3 to 4 tbsp. cooking oil. Cover and let cook on low heat until potatoes are half done. Remove lid and add chopped green onions, chopped white onions, celery, paprika and cut up wieners. Cover and cook on low heat until onions and celery are tender. Stir occasionally to keep potatoes from sticking to skillet.

CLARENCE

Rose L. Manasco
NATCHITOCHES PARISH

Fig Cake
SERVES 6-8

1 pint figs
1 cup flour
1/2 cup oil
2 eggs
1/2 cup nuts, chopped

Mix all ingredients. Bake in iron skillet in 325 degree oven until done. About 1 hour.

CLOUTIERVILLE

Maybell Carter
NATCHITOCHES PARISH

Chicken With Corn Bread Dressing
SERVES 12-15

1 4 to 5 lb. hen
4 cups corn bread crumbs
2 cups soft bread crumbs
1 cup green onions, chopped
1 1/2 cups celery, chopped
3 large onions, chopped
5 boiled eggs, chopped
4 raw eggs
Black pepper to taste
Salt to taste

Boil hen with salted water until tender (3 hours). Let cool in broth, then debone. Make a large iron skillet of corn bread using corn bread mix. Use the directions on package and crumble. Mix corn bread crumbs, soft bread crumbs, green onions, celery, chopped onions, and boiled eggs. Mix well, and add enough chicken broth to make mixture thin enough to pour easily. Add raw eggs and mix well. Pour into a roaster or large baking pan. Place chicken on top of dressing, but push it down into the dressing until it is just about covered. Cover with the roaster lid or foil and bake at 325 degrees for about 1 hour or longer if the baking dish is deep. The lid may have to be removed and the dressing browned under the broiler or cooked for a while without the lid until the desired color is reached.

COTTON VALLEY
Rebecca Holtzclaw
WEBSTER PARISH

Chicken Spaghetti

SERVES 4-6

1 chicken
1 bunch green onions, chopped
2 sticks celery, chopped
1 can cream of mushroom soup
1 can cream of celery soup
1/2 can cream of chicken soup
8 oz. sour cream
1 can Rotel tomatoes
1 bell pepper, sliced
1 small onion, sliced
1 small jar pimento
1 lb. Velveeta cheese
Spaghetti
Season to taste

Boil chicken with green onions and celery. Cool and remove from bone. Save broth to cook spaghetti. Mix the soups, sour cream, and Rotel tomatoes together and simmer over low heat. In a saucepan saute' the sliced bell pepper, onion and jar of pimentos. Boil spaghetti in broth and drain. Add soup mixture, sauteed vegetables and chicken together. Mix all together. Cut Velveeta into slices and put on top of mixture. Season to taste. Bake at 350 degrees for 15 or 20 minutes until cheese is melted.

COUSHATTA
Stephen Posey
RED RIVER PARISH

Chicken And Spaghetti
SERVES 8

1 large hen
3 cans tomato soup
1 stick oleo
2 large onions, chopped
1 package spaghetti
1/2 stalk celery, chopped
3 small bell peppers, chopped
2 tbsp. Worcestershire sauce
1 small bottle ketchup
Grated cheese for topping
Chili powder
Black pepper
Garlic salt

Cook hen and debone, reserving stock. Melt oleo and saute' onions, celery, and bell peppers until wilted but not brown. Add enough stock to cook until tender. Add tomato soup and other seasonings. Add chicken and as much stock as needed. Add this to the spaghetti that has been cooked. Spread grated cheese on. Bake only long enough to set. Delicious!

CULLEN

Ann Franks
WEBSTER PARISH

Red Dressing

YIELDS 1 QUART

1 cup oil
1/2 cup catsup
1/2 cup vinegar
1/2 cup sugar
2 tsp. onion salt
2 tsp. Worcestershire sauce

Mix all ingredients and chill. Stir well before using on any green salad.

DOYLINE

Don Griffith
WEBSTER PARISH

Liz's Rolls

MAKES 4 DOZEN

1 cup Crisco
1 cup sugar
1 tsp. salt
2 eggs
3 packages yeast
5 1/2 cups flour
2 cups water

Put 1 cup Crisco and 1 tsp. salt in a large bowl. Over this mixture pour 1 cup boiling water. Add 2 beaten eggs and stir together well. Add yeast dissolved in 1 cup warm water. Stir in all purpose flour (unsifted). Mix all together and refrigerate overnight. Put in greased muffin tins and let rise until double. Bake 425 degrees for 8 minutes.

DUBACH

Liz Trammel
LINCOLN PARISH

English Muffin Bread
SERVES 6

1 package active dry yeast
2 1/4 to 3 cups sifted all-purpose flour
1 1/2 cups water
1 tbsp. sugar
1/4 tsp. salt
Corn meal

In large mixer bowl, combine yeast and 1 cup of the flour. In medium saucepan heat water, sugar, and salt just till warm, stirring occasionally to dissolve sugar. Add to dry mixture in mixing bowl. Beat with electric mixer at low speed for 1/4 minute, scraping sides of bowl constantly. Beat 3 minutes at high speed. By hand stir in just enough of the remaining flour to make a soft dough. Place dough in lightly greased bowl; turn to grease surface. Cover; let rise in warm place till double, about 1 hour. Punch down. Cover; let rest 10 minutes. Grease a 1 1/4 quart casserole sprinkle with corn meal. Place dough in casserole sprinkle top with corn meal. Cover; let rise in warm place till double, about 45 to 60 minutes. Bake in hot 400 degree oven for 40 to 45 minutes or till done. (If top browns too fast, cover loosely with foil). Remove from dish to cool. Serve with butter.

GIBSLAND

Mrs. F. Lestar Martin
BIENVILLE PARISH

Doyle's Favorite

SERVES 6-8

1 onion, chopped
1 bell pepper, chopped
1 lb. smoked sausage
1 lb. chicken, boiled and deboned
1 lb. boiled shrimp (optional)
2 cans 8 oz. tomato sauce
1 can Rotel tomatoes with green chilies, chopped
3 cups of water to cover ingredients
Salt and pepper to taste

Saute' onion and bell pepper. Combine onion, bell pepper, sausage, chicken, shrimp, Rotel tomatoes, tomato sauce and water in large pot. Boil approximately 45 minutes. Serve over hot rice. Very good.......

GILLIAM

Rhonda Lawton Dauphin
CADDO PARISH

Cabbage Casserole
SERVES 10-12

1 medium head cabbage, coarsely chopped
2 cans whole tomatoes, including juice
2 small onions, chopped
2 medium size bell pepper, chopped
2 medium size potatoes, cubed
2 large carrots, cut in thin crosswise slices
1 12 1/2 oz. can white turkey meat, including liquid
1/2 tsp. crushed red pepper, to taste
Salt to taste
2 tbsp. soft margarine or bacon drippings
1/2 to 3/4 cups of water

Combine all ingredients in large pot on top of stove. Cook covered, until potatoes and carrots stick tender with fork. Let stand a few minutes in pot Remove to Pyrex casserole baking dish and reheat. Serve hot with hush puppies or corn bread sticks. NOTE: a little more water may be needed during cooking process. Other meat may be substituted for turkey, such as stuffed beef or pork sausage, chicken or ground chuck.

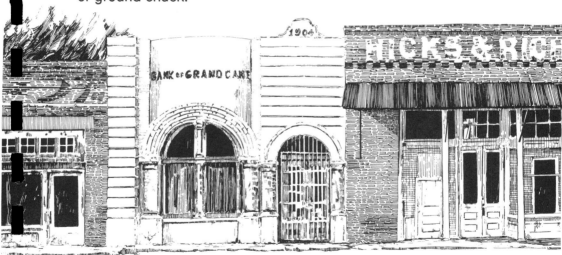

GRAND CANE

Lillie Mae McDuff
DESOTO PARISH

Marie's Art of Chili

SERVES 6

1/8 lb. deer burger
1 lb. venison, coarsely cubed
6 tbsp. chili powder
1/2 tsp. oregano
1 tsp. cumin seed
2 tsp. turmeric
1 tsp. cayenne

4 large garlic, minced
4 dried red chilies, broken up
2 Bay leaves
1 tsp. Tabasco sauce
1 1/2 quart water
1/2 cup corn meal or masa haring
1 tsp. salt

In Dutch oven, fry 1/8 lb. deer burger meat until brown. Add coarsely cut cubes of venison and brown. Add seasoning and water. Heat to boil. Reduce heat. Cover and simmer 1 1/2 hours. Skim fat off. Stir in corn meal or masa and simmer uncovered for 30 minutes. Stir occasionally. Can use venison, deer, ground turkey or ground beef.

GREENWOOD

Marie Brooks
CADDO PARISH

Squash Casserole

SERVES 4-6

3 cups squash, cooked
1 cup cheese, grated
2 eggs, beaten
1 onion, chopped
1 cup Ritz cracker crumbs
1 can cream of mushroom soup
Margarine
Salt and pepper to taste

Mix cooked squash, soup, onion, cheese, beaten eggs, salt and pepper and cracker crumbs. Pour into a buttered 1 1/2 quart casserole. Top with additional crushed cracker crumbs and dot with margarine. Bake at 350 degrees for 30 minutes or until golden brown.

HAUGHTON

Janie Fernandez
BOSSIER PARISH

Pineapple Cake

SERVES 20

1 1/2 cups sugar
2/3 cup oleo
2 cups flour
1 1/2 tsp. baking powder
1/4 tsp. soda
1 cup buttermilk
2 eggs
1 tsp. vanilla

Mix sugar and oleo. Add eggs. Then add buttermilk and flour (with soda and baking powder) alternately. End with flour mixture. Add vanilla. Bake in 9" X 13" pan for 30 minutes at 350 degrees.

PINEAPPLE ICING: Boil 1 15 1/2 oz. can crushed pineapple with juice, 1 1/4 cups sugar and 3 tbsp. flour until thick. Add 2 tbsp. oleo and dash of salt. Pat over cake while warm. After cake has cooled, ice with the following: 3/4 stick oleo and 3 tbsp. milk, brought to a boil. Add about 3 1/2 cups of powdered sugar and 1 tsp. vanilla. Pour on top of pineapple icing.

HAYNESVILLE

Tina B. Crocker
CLAIBORNE PARISH

220

Corn Pudding

SERVES 8-10

2 17 oz. cans cream style corn
1 large onion, chopped
2/3 cup green pepper, chopped
1 cup uncooked instant rice
1 small jar pimento
1 stick oleo
1 tbsp. brown sugar
Salt and pepper to taste

Saute' onion and pepper in oleo. Add all other ingredients.
Mix well and pour into casserole dish. Bake 1 hour at 350
degrees.

HODGE

Selwyn G. Johnson
JACKSON PARISH

Chicken Spaghetti

SERVES 8-10

1 stewing hen	1 large jar pimento
1 large bell pepper, chopped	1 lb. Hoop cheese, grated
2 medium onions, chopped	1 large package spaghetti
2 cups celery, chopped	Tabasco sauce
1 garlic button, chopped	Salt
1 can tomato paste	Pepper
1/2 stick margarine	

Chop vegetables and saute' in margarine. Boil and debone hen. Reduce broth to 2 quarts. Add chicken and vegetables to broth. Add pimento. Cook spaghetti in salted water until about half done. Drain and add to sauce. Bring to a simmer and add 1/2 of the cheese. Season to taste and place in large baking dish. Spread remaining grated cheese on top and bake for 30 minutes in 350 degree oven.

HOMER

Kathyrn Martin
CLAIBORNE PARISH

Chocolate Sheath Cake

SERVES 25

1 stick margarine
1 cup water
2 eggs
3 1/2 tbsp. cocoa
2 cups flour
1/2 cup buttermilk
1/2 cup Crisco
2 cups sugar
1 tsp. soda
1 tsp. vanilla

Put in saucepan and bring to boil the margarine, cocoa and Crisco. Pour over sugar and flour. Add eggs, buttermilk, soda, vanilla and mix well. Bake in a well greased oblong pan for about 20 minutes at 400 degrees. ICING: 5 minutes before cake is done mix 3 1/2 tsp. cocoa, 1/2 cup milk and 1 stick margarine. Bring to a boil. Add 1 package powder sugar. Mix well and pour over hot cake.

HOSSTON

Louise Crowley
CADDO PARISH

223

Potato Casserole
SERVES 12

1 large onion, chopped
1 bell pepper, chopped (optional)
1 lb. Velveeta cheese
1 pint sour cream, 2 cartons
1 can cream of mushroom soup
1 2 lb. package frozen hash brown potatoes
Salt and pepper to taste

Saute' onion and bell pepper in butter or oleo. Add cheese
and melt. Remove from heat and add sour cream and soup.
Mix with partially thawed potatoes and bake 1 1/2 hours at
325 degrees. Stir every 30 minutes. Use large pyrex dish.
OK to add pimento if you like.

JONESBORO

Floy Cox
JACKSON PARISH

Fresh Broccoli Salad

SERVES 6

1 bunch broccoli
1 small red onion, chopped
4 or 5 slices crumbled bacon (optional)
1/2 cup raisins
1/4 to 1/3 cup vinegar
1 1/2 tbsp. sugar
Black pepper to taste
3/4 cup mayonnaise (NOT salad dressing)

Wash and drain Broccoli. Peel stems of broccoli and dice into small pieces. Separate flowerettes. Add onions, bacon and raisins. DRESSING: Combine last four ingredients and whip with wire whisk until smooth and creamy. Amounts of vinegar and sugar may be adjusted to taste. Pour dressing over broccoli and let set 2 to 3 hours before serving.

KEATCHIE

Betty Shows
DESOTO PARISH

Cream Cheese Pound Cake
SERVES 10-12

1/2 cup butter type shortening
1/2 cup real butter
2 8 oz. packages of cream cheese
3 cups sugar
6 eggs
3 cups self rising flour
1 1/2 tsp. vanilla extract
1 tsp. lemon extract

Grease and flour a 10" tube pan and preheat oven to 325 degrees. Cream shortening, real butter and cream cheese. Add sugar and cream real well, at least 3 to 4 minutes at medium speed. Add eggs, 1 at a time, alternating with flour. Add extracts and mix well. Bake at 325 degrees for 1 1/2 hours or until toothpick inserted in center comes out clean.

MANSFIELD

Nelda Laffitte
DESOTO PARISH

Dot's Shrimp

SERVES 6-8

10 lbs. shrimp (heads off)
1 large bottle Italian salad dressing
1 lb. Parkay oleo
1 medium bottle lemon juice
5 or 6 lemons, sliced
2 to 4 oz. black pepper
Salt to taste

Mix and cook in a Dutch oven covered for 45 minutes at 350 degrees. Stir occasionally. Serve in soup bowl with juice and eat with French bread. "Very good!"

MANY

Billie Lou Luster
SABINE PARISH

Shrimp DeBarbara
SERVES 4-6

Onion, chopped
Green pepper, chopped
Celery, chopped
Butter
Shrimp, peeled
1 cup white wine
Salt
Pepper
Tony Chachere's seasoning
Flour

Chop equal amounts of onion, green pepper, celery and saute' in butter until golden. Add raw peeled medium size shrimp. Stir until shrimp are pink. Add 1 cup white wine, salt, pepper and Tony Chachere's to taste. Simmer several minutes, then sprinkle with flour. " I serve this over white rice, but would be equally good on puffed pastry shells for a light luncheon dish."

MINDEN

Barbara Simmons
WEBSTER PARISH

Harvest Festival Stew

SERVES 52

3 lbs. beef	SAUCE:
1 lb. pork	1/2 tsp. oregano
1 hen	1 tsp. marjoram
5 lbs. potatoes, diced	1 tsp. sweet basil
2 lbs. carrots, sliced	2 tsp. parsley
4 large onions, chopped	2 tsp. paprika
1 stalk celery, diced	1/2 tsp. celery seed
3 bell peppers, diced	1 tsp. dry mustard
8 cloves garlic, minced	2 tbsp. chili powder
16 oz. can tomato juice	1 can condensed tomato
16 oz. can tomatoes	soup
16 oz. can corn	1 tbsp. brown sugar
16 oz. can English peas	2 tbsp. horseradish
Salt and pepper to taste	1/2 cup catsup

In large 4 gallon stew pot place hen in enough water to cover (approximately 2 quarts) and cook until tender. Remove hen from pot and debone. While chicken is cooking cut up beef and pork and sear lightly in a large skillet with enough vegetable oil to keep from sticking. Cook beef and pork in chicken broth until tender. Add vegetables and cook till tender. Add deboned chicken and sauce. Simmer. ONE HOUR BEFORE SERVING add one cup sour cream and one cup of cheddar cheese in one cup of thin white sauce.

MOORINGSPORT

Jeannie Moore
CADDO PARISH

Donna's Chicken Casserole
SERVES 15

2 chickens
1 stalk celery, chopped
1 bell pepper, chopped
2 onions, chopped
1/2 cup butter
1 small can ripe olives, chopped
1 small jar pimento, chopped
2 cans cream of chicken soup
2 cups Cheddar cheese, grated
1 package spaghetti
1 tsp. garlic powder
Salt and pepper to taste

Cook chicken, cool and debone. Save broth. Saute' onions, celery, and bell pepper in butter. Boil spaghetti in reserved chicken broth. Drain. Mix all ingredients and pour into large casserole dish. Sprinkle 1/2 cup of grated cheese on top and bake for 30 minutes at 350 degrees.

MT. LEBANON

Donna Towns
BIENVILLE PARISH

230

Pizza Bread
SERVES 10

1 10 to 12 oz. Mozzarella cheese, shredded
1 small can of ripe olives, chopped
4 green onions, chopped, tops included
1 stick of oleo
1/2 cup mayonnaise
Sprinkle of garlic salt
French bread

Melt the oleo in a large saucepan. Add the cheese, olives,
green onions, mayonnaise and garlic salt. Mix well. Put this
mixture on regular sliced bread, French bread, or leftover rolls
which have been sliced. Broil in a 375 degree oven and
watch carefully. It will be done when it begins to brown, about
5 minutes. It is also great on homemade sliced bread. This
mixture will keep in the refrigerator for 3 to 4 weeks.

NATCHEZ

Martha D. Lane
NATCHITOCHES PARISH

Meat Pies

MAKES 18

FILLING:
1 tsp. shortening
1 lb. ground meat
1 lb. ground pork
1 bunch green onions, chopped
1 pod garlic, minced
1 bell pepper, chopped
Salt, black and red pepper to taste
1 tbsp. flour

CRUST:
1 quart plain flour
2 tsp. salt
1 tsp. baking powder
1 egg
1/2 cup shortening
1 cup milk

Melt shortening in heavy pot. Add meat and seasonings which have been chopped into small pieces. Stir often. When meat is done but not dry, remove from heat. Stir in 1 tbsp. flour.

Sift dry ingredients together. Cut in shortening. Beat egg and add to milk. Work gradually into dry ingredients until proper consistency to roll. Break into small pieces and roll very thin. Cut into rounds using a saucer as a guide. To assemble: Place a large tbsp. of prepared meat along edge and halfway in the center of round dough. Fold the other half over, making edges meet. Firm edges with fork. Drop in deep fat and cook until golden brown. Drain and serve hot.

NATCHITOCHES

Gay Melder
NATCHITOCHES PARISH

Ambrosia Supreme Cake

SERVES 12-16

1 lemon supreme cake mix,
Duncan Hines
4 eggs
1/2 cup vegetable oil
1 11 oz. can Mandarin
Oranges, undrained
1 tbsp. orange rind, grated
1 tbsp. Amaretto

ICING:
1 small can coconut
1 10 oz. package no-bake
cheesecake filling, Jello
Brand
1 12 oz. Cool Whip
1/4 cup Amaretto
1 tbsp. sugar
1 20 oz. can undrained
crushed pineapple

Preheat oven to 325 degrees. Mix all cake ingredients. Pour in 4 (9 inch) pans. Bake for 15 to 20 minutes. Let cool in pans.

For ICING: mix all ingredients except Cool Whip. Fold in Cool Whip after mixing other ingredients. Spread between layers and over cake. Refrigerate.

OIL CITY

June Eaton
CADDO PARISH

Pumpkin Cheesecake

SERVES 8-10

1/3 cup margarine
1/3 cup sugar
1 egg
1 1/4 cups flour
2 8 oz. packages of
 Philadelphia Brand cream cheese
3/4 cup sugar

16 oz. can pumpkin
1 tsp. cinnamon
1/4 tsp. ginger
1/4 tsp. nutmeg
Dash of salt
2 eggs

Using first 4 ingredients. Cream margarine and sugar until light and fluffy. Blend in the egg. Add flour and mix well. Press dough on bottom and 2 inches high around sides of a 9 inch spring form pan. Bake at 400 degrees for 5 minutes. Reduce oven temperature to 350 degrees. Combine softened cream cheese and sugar, mixing at medium speed on electric mixer until well blended. Blend in pumpkin, spices and salt and mix well. Add eggs one at a time mixing well after each addition. Pour mixture into pastry lined pan and smooth surface to edge of crust. Bake at 350 degrees for 50 minutes. Loosen cake from rim of pan. Cool before removing rim of pan. Chill. Garnish with whipped cream just before serving, if desired.

PLAIN DEALING

Judie Barnette
BOSSIER PARISH

Hobo Supper
SERVES 8

16 chicken thighs or choice of chicken parts OR
2 lbs. hamburger formed into thick patties
8 medium potatoes, peeled and quartered
1 lb. carrots, peeled and sliced
2 stalks celery, peeled and cut in 1/2" slices
1 sweet pepper, cut in rings
1 onion, chopped
1 medium cabbage, cut in wedges
6 slices bacon
1/2 lb. boneless ham, cubed
1 envelope Lipton onion soup mix
Salt and pepper to taste

Preheat oven to 350 degrees. Line 10" x 16" x 3" baking pan
with foil, leaving extra to extend well over top of pan. Place
chicken, skin side down in pan. Layer potatoes, carrots,
celery, pepper and cabbage randomly over chicken. Season
with salt and pepper as desired. Top all with onion rings and
cubed ham. Sprinkle onion soup mix over all. Place bacon
slices across top. Cover with foil and seal completely. (Do
Not add any liquid, as in cooking, it will make its own.) Bake
approximately 2 1/2 hours or until vegetables are tender.

PLEASANT HILL
Mickey Veuleman
SABINE PARISH

Corn Bread Dressing
SERVES 30

3 fryers or 1 fat hen
2 large onions, chopped
1 stalk celery, chopped
2 pones corn bread (9" X 12" cake pan)
1/2 lb. crackers
8 boiled eggs
1 stick oleo
1 or 2 cans jellied cranberry sauce
Salt and pepper to taste

Boil chicken (should have plenty of broth). Chop onions and celery and saute' them in skillet using one stick oleo. Crumble up your corn bread and crackers in a large bowl or in a dishpan (the dishpan works better as this makes a lot of dressing). Add boiled eggs and broth from your chicken. Mix all of these ingredients together and pour into a large roaster pan. Bake at 450 degrees until golden brown. Serve cranberry sauce with dressing.

PROVENCAL

Eula Bates
NATCHITOCHES PARISH

Hot Shrimp
SERVES 3-5

4 lbs. shrimp
Wishbone Italian dressing
Pepper, cracked or coarse ground
1 lb. butter

Wash fresh shrimp. Cover with dressing and marinate over-night in covered container in refrigerator. Drain shrimp, leaving wet with dressing. Place in large baking pan. Cover with butter and pepper. Use pepper liberally. Bake 45 minutes (or less depending on oven) in 400 degree oven. Stir Occasionally.

RINGGOLD

Roselyn Causey
BIENVILLE PARISH

Home Made Bread
MAKES 2 LOAVES

4 cups flour
2 cups warm water
1 egg
3 tbsp. vegetable oil
6 tbsp. sugar
1/2 tsp. salt
1 package yeast

Dissolve yeast in warm water and set aside. Mix oil, egg, sugar and salt in large bowl. Add yeast and water mixture and mix. Slowly add flour until you have a stiff dough. Knead a few minutes and roll into a ball. Let rise about 1 1/2 to 2 hours. Punch down and separate into muffin pans or loaf pans.

ROBELINE
Johnnie Thigpen
NATCHITOCHES PARISH

Rodessa Trail Riders Chili

SERVES 15-20 HUNGRY TRAIL RIDERS

4 packages stew meat
1 package pork ribs
6 lbs. chili meat
1 lb. bacon, chopped
2 cans hot chili peppers
3 bell peppers, chopped
3 large onions, chopped
1 can tomato paste

3 cans stewed tomaotes
Ranch Style Beans
Black pepper
Salt
Chili powder
Garlic
Cayenne pepper
Cumin

In a large pot add stew meat, pork ribs, chili meat and chopped bacon. Cook until pork falls from bones and stew meat is tender. Remove bones. Add seasoning and remaining ingredients, except beans and cook about 2 hours on low fire. Add beans the last 20 minutes of cooking. Serve with crackers or over rice.

RODESSA

Regenia B. Gryder
CADDO PARISH

Sarah's Hot-Water Bread
SERVES 8-10

4 cups of water
2 cups corn meal
2 tsp. salt

Add corn meal and salt to boiling water. Stir well, until all the lumps are gone. Mold into patties (about 2 1/2" by 2") or pones. Fry in 1 inch vegetable oil until brown, then turn. Brown again, about 4 minutes each side.

RUSTON

Sarah Albritton/Sarah's Kitchen
LINCOLN PARISH

Fried Hot Water Bread
SERVES 8-10

1 cup corn meal
1/2 cup flour
1 tsp. salt
1 tsp. baking powder

Mix dry ingredients well and add boiling water. Make consistency of hamburger patties. Make into patties and fry in hot fat.

SALINE

Barbara A. Nutt
BIENVILLE PARISH

Chili

SERVES 6-8

2 lbs. ground chuck
1/4 cup onion, chopped
2 cans chili hot beans (optional)
2 cans tomato sauce
1 can Rotel tomatoes
2 cups water
2 tbsp. chili powder
1 tsp. salt

Brown meat and onions. Drain. Add rest of ingredients and bring to boil. Simmer (the longer the better).

SAREPTA

Johniece Whitehead
WEBSTER PARISH

Coconut Caramel Pie
SERVES 16

1/4 cup oleo
1 7 oz. package coconut
1/2 cup pecans, chopped
1 8 oz. package cream cheese
1 14 oz. can condensed milk
1 16 oz. container Cool Whip
2 Graham cracker crusts
1 12 oz. jar caramel ice cream topping

Melt oleo in skillet. Add coconut and nuts and cook until brown. Combine cream cheese and milk. Beat until smooth then fold in Cool Whip. Layer in Graham cracker crust, cream cheese mixture, caramel topping and coconut and pecan mixture.
REPEAT cream cheese, caramel topping coconut mixture. Makes 2 - 9" pies. Store in freezer until 5 minutes before serving, then cut. Very rich.

SHONGALOO

Idelle Simms
WEBSTER PARISH

Caesar Salad

SERVES 6

1 cup croutons
Olive oil
1 clove garlic
6 cups Romaine lettuce, split
1 egg
Juice of 1 lemon
1/2 cup Parmesan cheese, grated
Fresh ground pepper
1 tsp. salt

Brown croutons in oil in skillet. Rub wooden salad bowl with garlic, add Romaine. Pour 1/4 cup olive oil over Romaine lettuce. Add salt, pepper and toss gently. Break egg into center of bowl and squeeze lemon. Stir egg and juice until creamy.   Toss with Romaine and add cheese. Mix again and add croutons. Serve immediately.

SHREVEPORT
Gay Verges
CADDO PARISH

Meat Loaf

SERVES 8

2 lbs. ground beef
1 tall can evaporated milk
2 tbsp. Worcestershire sauce
1 cup bread crumbs
1/2 cup onion, chopped fine
1/2 cup catsup or chili sauce
2 tsp. salt
1/2 tsp. pepper
French Provincial Herbs to taste

Mix all ingredients together. Shape into loaf in center of 9" x
13" x 2" baking pan. Bake at 350 degrees about 1 hour and
15 minutes or until well browned. Allow meat loaf to stand 10
minutes for easier slicing. Delicious served either hot or cold.

SIMSBORO

Ruth Alexander
LINCOLN PARISH

Squirrel Mulligan

SERVES 12

3 squirrels
1 chicken
1/2 lb. bacon, chopped
1/2 lb. butter
3 onions, chopped
2 bell peppers, chopped
1 10 oz package spaghetti
1 can English peas

2 cans Mexicorn
2 cans tomatoes
1 bottle ketchup
1/2 bottle Tabasco
Salt and cayenne pepper to taste
2 tbsp. celery salt
2 tbsp. chili powder

Boil meat and debone. Save broth. Brown chopped bacon in skillet. Remove bacon. Add butter to bacon grease. Add chopped onions and bell pepper and cook about 10 or 15 minutes. In a large stock pot mix all ingredients together. Add English peas, Mexicorn, tomatoes, ketchup, Tabasco, cayenne pepper, celery salt and chili powder. Salt to taste. Simmer 2 hours. Add spaghetti 30 minutes before serving.

SPRINGHILL

Kathy Shaver
WEBSTER PARISH

Chicken And Seafood Gumbo
SERVES 6-8

6 tbsp. shortening
6 tbsp. flour
1 onion, minced
1/4 cup celery, diced
1 green pepper, chopped
1 cup parsley
2 tbsp. salt
2 tbsp. black pepper
1/2 tsp. gumbo file'
1 chicken, cut in serving pieces
2 dozen oysters
1 lb. shrimp
Crabs

Heat shortening on high, add flour and stir constantly until brown. This brown fat and flour is a roux. Add onions, celery and other vegetables until wilted. Add 6 cups of hot water. Mix well to dissolve roux. Season with salt and pepper. Bring to a boil, switch to a low heat and cook until chicken is tender (about 2 hours). Then add oysters, shrimp, and crabs. Let cook for 15 more minutes. Add file'. Serve over rice.

VIENNA

DeCinter C. Farley
LINCOLN PARISH

Sausage Bread

SERVES 8-12

3 loaves frozen bread
1 lb. smoked sausage
1 6 oz. can tomato paste
Red pepper
Black pepper

Thaw bread and roll out each loaf. Spread portion of tomato paste on each loaf (thin). Sprinkle with both peppers, then place sliced smoked sausage. Fold each loaf. Bake at 350 degrees until brown. Option: for pizza bread and children, leave off peppers, add garlic and shredded cheese, any meat substitute will do. Very easy and delicious.

VIVIAN

Diann House
CADDO PARISH

Half Pound Cake

SERVES 6-8

1 cup margarine
1 1/2 cups sugar
4 eggs, separated
2 cups all purpose flour
1 tsp. baking powder
1/2 cup milk
1 tsp. vanilla
1 tsp. lemon extract

Cream margarine. Then add sugar slowly and cream well. Add egg yolks one at a time and beat. Add flour sifted with baking powder alternately with milk. Beat well. Add flavorings, then fold in stiffly beaten egg whites. Bake in oven at 350 degrees for about 45 minutes. Makes 1 loaf cake.

WINNFIELD

Mrs. Gay Baker
WINN PARISH

Hot Tamales
MAKES 30 DOZEN

DOUGH:
5 lbs. Masa Harina
1/3 cup salt
1/4 cup garlic salt
4 1/4 quart broth
1 1/2 cup pork lard

MEAT:
16 lbs. pork
1/4 cup salt
1/4 cup garlic salt
1/4 cup black pepper
Crushed red pepper
30 dozen corn shucks

Boil the meat until tender. Grind meat fine and add salt, garlic salt, black and red pepper to taste. Stir with large spoon until all ingredients are mixed well. Now mix the dough. Pour in large bowl the Masa Harina and add salt, garlic salt and broth from the meat. Stir until smooth. Soak corn shucks in hot water until soft, then drain. With a knife spread a thin layer of dough about 2 inches across the shuck and about 2 inches from the bottom. Then spread about 2 tbsp. of meat mixture down the side of the dough. Roll shuck and fold up end. Place in a pot with folded end down. Add from 2 to 3 cups water and steam for 1 hour.

ZWOLLE

Dorothy L. Leone
SABINE PARISH

Northeast Section

Alto
Baskin
Bastrop
Bernice
Clarks
Clayton
Columbia
Crowville
Delhi
Epps
Farmerville
Ferriday
Forest
Gilbert
Grayson

Harrisonburg
Jena
Jonesville
Junction City
Lake Providence
Mangham
Marion
Mer Rouge
Monroe
Mound
Newellton
Oak Grove
Oak Ridge
Olla

Rayville
Sicily Island
Sondheimer
St. Joseph
Tallulah
Transylvania
Tullos
Urania
Vidalia
Waterproof
West Monroe
Winnsboro
Wisner

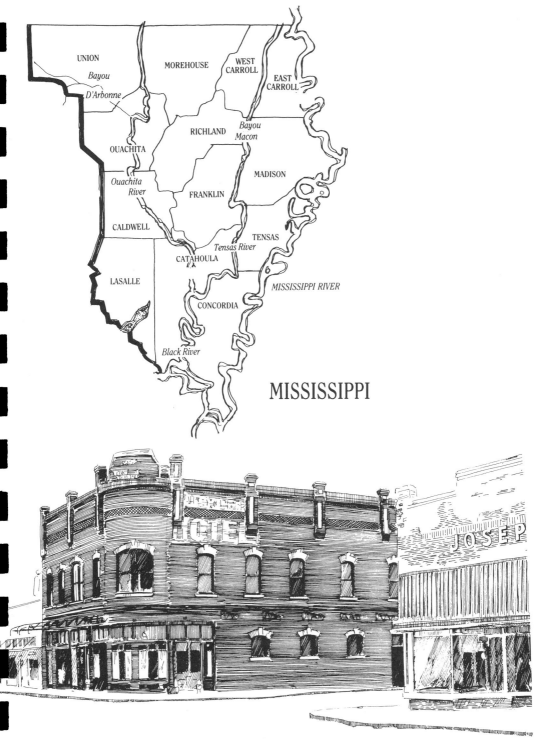

UNION

Bayou
D'Arbonne

MOREHOUSE

WEST
CARROLL

EAST
CARROLL

RICHLAND

Bayou
Macon

OUACHITA

Ouachita
River

FRANKLIN

MADISON

CALDWELL

TENSAS

Tensas River

CATAHOULA

LASALLE

MISSISSIPPI RIVER

CONCORDIA

Black River

MISSISSIPPI

253

Rolls
MAKES 48

1 cup warm water
1 package (1/4 oz.) yeast
1 tsp. sugar
6 cups flour
1 cup milk
2 tsp. salt
5 tbsp. sugar
4 tbsp. melted shortening

Combine water and 1 teaspoon sugar. Sprinkle in package of yeast. Heat milk to scalding; cool some and then add to mixture. Add salt, sugar, 3 cups flour and melted shortening. Beat and beat (this is the secret). Then add 3 cups of flour or more if needed. Knead. Let rise until double or about one hour. Punch down, turn over. Cover and let rise 1 1/2 hours. Roll and let rise about 40 minutes. Brush tops of rolls with melted butter before baking. Bake at 400 degrees until brown.

ALTO

Eula Lee Pardue
RICHLAND PARISH

Rice-A-Roni Salad

SERVES 8-10

1 box chicken Rice-A-Roni
1 jar marinated artichoke hearts
1 chicken breast cooked or
1 can chicken (small)
5-6 green onions
1/2 cup mayonnaise
1/4 cup bell pepper
Water chestnuts (optional)
1/2 tsp. salt
1/2 tsp. pepper

Cook Rice-A-Roni according to package directions - cool - add chopped onions, chopped bell pepper, chopped artichoke hearts and chopped chicken. Mix mayonnaise with reserved marinade from artichokes and add to rice. Mix well - chill-serve on lettuce leaf. You can add more chicken and have a real nice luncheon salad.

BASKIN

Ann Thompson
FRANKLIN PARISH

Broccoli And Cheese Soup
SERVES 8

2 packages chopped frozen broccoli
2 stalks celery, chopped
1 large onion, chopped
1 stick butter
3 cans cream of mushroom soup
1 jar whole button mushrooms
1 quart milk
1 tbsp. Accent
1 roll jalapeno cheese
8 ozs. Velveeta cheese
1 tbsp. soy sauce
1 tbsp. Tony's Creole seasoning

Saute' onions, celery and mushrooms in butter. Cook broccoli as directed. Add soup to sauteed vegetables, then add cheese, slowly add milk after cheese has melted. Stir frequently and add remaining ingredients. Let simmer on low heat for 30-45 minutes until done. Serve with crackers or corn bread.

BASTROP

Rosemary Brumfield
MOREHOUSE PARISH

Creamy Corn Pudding

SERVES 6

6 tbsp. flour
6 tbsp. butter
4 tbsp. sugar
1 1/2 tsp. salt
1 1/2 cup milk
2 (17 oz.) cans cream style corn
6 eggs

Melt butter in heavy saucepan over low heat. Add flour, sugar and salt, stirring until smooth. Cook one minute stirring constantly. Gradually add milk. Cook over medium heat stirring constantly until thickened. Remove mixture from heat and stir in corn. Beat eggs well. Gradually stir about 1/4 of hot mixture into beaten eggs. Add to remaining hot mixture stirring constantly. Pour into buttered casserole. Bake at 350 degrees for one hour. (Check at 45 minutes. Sometimes it is done.)

BERNICE

Mrs. Loy Reeder
UNION PARISH

Ambrosia Salad
SERVES 6

1 large can crushed pineapple
8 oranges (peeled and cubed)
2 packages frozen coconut
1 cup chopped pecans
Sugar

In salad bowl layer pineapple, oranges, coconut and pecans.
Cover with sugar and repeat until all ingredients are used.
Cover and chill in refrigerator over night.

CLARKS
Patsy Taylor
CALDWELL PARISH

Cheese Grits
SERVES 6-8

1 cup grits
1/4 cup butter
3 eggs
1/2 lb. sharp cheese
Salt to taste
Sprinkle with red pepper

Cook grits as directed on box. Add ingredients as listed, beating hard after each addition. Bake at 325-350 degrees for 1 hour.

CLAYTON

Nancy R. Anders
CONCORDIA PARISH

Hickory Smoked Turkey

SERVES 25-30

1 large turkey (16 to 18 lbs.)
Salt
Pepper

Place seasoned turkey on rack in large baking pan and bake at 325 degrees until about 3/4 done. Place a foil tent over the turkey to keep it from browning. Build a large charcoal fire on one end of barbecue barrel. After coals are grey, add 6 or 8 wet hickory chips to top of coals. Place partially cooked turkey on opposite end (away from coals). Close barrel and cook for several hours, basting with glaze every 30 minutes, until turkey is golden brown and done.
(APRICOT HONEY GLAZE: 1 12 oz. can apricot nectar, 1 12 oz. jar honey, 1 cup turkey drippings, 1 tsp. salt. Heat together in 2 quart sauce pan.)

COLUMBIA

Edgar W. Duke/Assessor 1951-80
CALDWELL PARISH

Sweet Potato Cheesecake
SERVES 12-15

1 16 oz. package yellow cake mix
3 eggs
2 tbsp. melted butter
4 tsp. pumpkin pie spice
1 8 oz. container cream cheese (softened)
1 14 oz. can sweetened condensed milk
2 cups mashed sweet potatoes
1 tsp. cinnamon
1/2 tsp. salt
1 cup chopped pecans
Whip cream or Cool Whip

In small mixing bowl combine cake mix, 1 egg, butter and 2 tsp. of spice. Beat on low speed until crumbly. Press in bottom of 9" X 13" baking pan. Set aside. In large mixing bowl, beat cream cheese until fluffy. Add condensed milk, 2 eggs, 2 tsp. spice, sweet potatoes, cinnamon and salt and mix until blended. Pour into crust and sprinkle with nuts. Bake at 350 degrees for 30-40 minutes or until set. Cool - refrigerate until ready to serve. To serve cut into squares and top with whipped cream or Cool Whip.

CROWVILLE
Mrs. Julia Nelson
FRANKLIN PARISH

"Quick" Hot Tamales
MAKES 4 DOZEN

2 1/2 lbs. ground beef or deer meat
2 medium onions
2 tsp. salt
4 cloves garlic
6 tbsp. chili powder

2 tbsp. Chili-O (French's)
1/2 cup water
1 1/2 cup tomato sauce
1/2 can Rotel tomatoes
1/4 tsp. red pepper
48 corn shucks

Clean and simmer corn shucks in water, then let drain. In a blender, blend all the ingredients. Add blended ingredients to 2 1/2 lbs. ground beef or deer meat. To make tamales -put 3 3/4 cups corn meal, 1 tbsp. salt, 1 tbsp. chili powder in large pan. Sprinkle meal mixture on shucks. Place a portion of meat mixture on shucks, roll, turning ends in to enclose meat mixture. Stand tamales up close together in steamer. Pour mixture of 1 1/2 cup tomato sauce, 1 tsp. salt, 2 tbsp. chili powder, 1 package plus remainder of Chili-O from meat mixture and 1/2 can Rotel tomatoes over tamales. Add enough water to cover tamales. Steam for 2 hours or longer. Set lid so steam escapes. Remove tamales and season juice with cumin, chili powder and bullion cubes. Thicken with flour (according to amount of liquid). Pour back over tamales.

DELHI
Suzybelle Hopson
RICHLAND PARISH

Green Noodles And Chicken
SERVES 8

4-5 chicken breasts
1 package green noodles
1 large can sliced mushrooms
1/2 lb. Velveeta cheese
1 can mushroom soup
1 small bottle stuffed olives
1 cup celery, chopped
1 cup onion, chopped
1/2 cup bell pepper, chopped
1/2 stick oleo
Salt to taste
Pepper to taste

Simmer breasts in salted water. Boil noodles in stock from breasts letting them absorb the stock. Saute' celery, onion and bell pepper in oleo. Add cheese and stir until melted. Add soup, mushrooms and olives. Mix this with the noodles and deboned chicken which has been cut up. Bake in greased casserole for 1 hour at 350 degrees.

EPPS
Marion Love Patton
WEST CARROLL PARISH

Chicken Pie

SERVES 6-8

1 large fryer or hen,
  seasoned with salt and pepper
8 hard boiled eggs
3 cups plain flour
Salt
Pepper

Cover chicken with water, cook until bones are easily removed. Salt and pepper chicken while cooking, have plenty
broth. PASTRY: Mix 3 cups flour with just enough hot broth to
make a stiff dough. (The warm dough is very easy to handle).
Cover bottom of baking pan with 1/2 deboned chicken. Chop 4
eggs and cover with broth. Cover with thin strips of dough.
Bake in 350 degree oven until golden brown. Repeat process,
add oleo bake until light brown.

FARMERVILLE

Gloria S. Moon
UNION PARISH

Trifling Trifle

SERVES 12

1 large Sara Lee pound cake, thawed and cut into 1/2" slices
Enough bourbon to moisten cake slices
1 pint whipping cream, whipped
1 large package instant vanilla pie filling, prepared as
   instructed on package or you may use your own boiled
   custard recipe
2 16 oz. frozen strawberries, undrained
1 20 oz. can crushed pineapple, drained
1 10 oz. jar Maraschino cherries, drained and chopped
   (reserve 5 or 6 to top Trifle)
1 6 oz. package frozen coconut, thawed

Mix last three ingredients together and set aside. Place 5 or 6
tbsp. of juice from strawberries in bottom of Trifle
bowl. Arrange cake slices, which have been sprinkled with
bourbon, over strawberry juice. Cut cake to fit so that
bottom of bowl is covered. Spoon 1/2 of strawberries over
cake. Cover strawberries with 1/2 of whipped cream. Layer
bourbon-moistened cake slices over whipped cream. Spoon
pineapple, coconut, and cherry mixture over cake. Spread
custard over this mixture. Cover with bourbon-sprinkled cake
slices. Spoon in rest of strawberries. Finish with
remaining whipped cream and garnish with whole cherries.
Cover and refrigerate overnight. This fills a 8" X 5 1/2"
Trifle bowl.

FERRIDAY

Mrs. Gene Tumminello
CONCORDIA PARISH

Old Fashioned Sweet Potato Pone
SERVES 6

3 cups grated raw sweet potatoes
1 cup sweet milk
1 1/2 cups sugar
2 eggs
1 tbsp. butter
1 tsp. allspice
1 tsp. cinnamon

Mix all ingredients thoroughly. Pour into well-greased heated iron skillet. Cook in a moderate oven until brown and until the sweet potato begins to leave the sides of the skillet.

FOREST
Kayla Tindell Sevier
WEST CARROLL PARISH

Marinated Mixed Vegetables

SERVES 4

1 cup Laseur peas
1 cup tiny white corn
1 small jar pimentos
1 medium onion, minced
3 stalks celery, sliced thin
1 medium bell pepper, minced

Mix vegetables and marinate in 1 cup vinegar, 1/2 cup oil
and 1 1/2 cup sugar.

GILBERT

Harriet Wilcher
FRANKLIN PARISH

Bread Pudding and Rum Sauce
SERVES 8-10

1 stick oleo	RUM SAUCE
1 1/2 cups sugar	1 cup milk
3 eggs	1 cup evaporated milk
1 15 oz. can Pet milk	3 tbsp. corn starch
1 1/2 cups water	3 tbsp. butter
6 slices white bread	1/2 cup sugar
1 tbsp. vanilla	1 to 3 oz. rum

Melt oleo, add sugar and mix. Add eggs one at a time mixing after each. Add milk and water and mix well. Tear up 6 slices of bread and punch down in liquid. Add vanilla, it sometimes looks like clabber. Pour into a 9" X 13" baking dish. Sprinkle over top with a mixture of 2 tbsp. of sugar, 1 tsp. cinnamon, and 1 tsp. nutmeg. Bake at 350 degrees for 25 to 30 minutes. RUM SAUCE: Heat the two milks with butter and sugar, add the corn starch mixed with a small amount of water. Cook and stir until thick. Remove from fire, add rum and stir well. Serve over bread pudding either hot or cold.

GRAYSON
Billie Howell
CALDWELL PARISH

Mrs. Jean E.'s Frosted Oatmeal Cookies
MAKES 5 DOZEN COOKIES

1 cup butter, softened
1 cup brown sugar, packed
1 cup granulated sugar
2 eggs
1 tsp. vanilla
1 1/2 cups all purpose flour
1 tsp. soda
1 tsp. salt
3 cups quick cooking oatmeal

Cream the softened butter (or margarine) and the sugars. Add eggs and blend. Add vanilla, then the dry ingredients. Add the uncooked oatmeal last. Chill dough overnight in refrigerator or freezer. When dough is cold, roll into balls (2 tsps. dough per ball). Place 12 balls on a cookie sheet (ungreased sheet). Bake at 375 degrees for about 10 minutes. Cookies will spread . Remove immediately from sheet when done. Cool cookies on waxed paper. Brush on frosting when cookies are cooled. CINNAMON COFFEE FROSTING: 3 tbsp. melted butter, 1 cup powdered sugar, 1 tbsp. liquid coffee, 1 tsp. vanilla and 1/2 tsp. cinnamon. Mix and brush on cooled cookies.

HARRISONBURG
Jean E. Mitchell
CATAHOULA PARISH

Broccoli Soup
SERVES 6

1 stick oleo
4-5 green onions
1/2 cup flour
2 cups milk
1 roll garlic cheese,
  cut into chunks
3/4 to 1 roll jalapeno cheese,
  cut into chunks
2 boxes chopped broccoli
2-3 cans chicken broth

Cook the two boxes of broccoli according to package directions - drain. Saute green onions in melted oleo. Add flour - cook about 1 minute or until smooth. Add milk slowly. Add garlic and jalapeno cheeses. Cook and stir until melted. Add broccoli and chicken broth. Heat thoroughly.

JENA

Tasca Dean
LA SALLE PARISH

Angel Biscuits

SERVES 15-20

1 package yeast
2 tbsp. sugar
1/2 cup hot tap water
5 cups self-rising flour
1 cup shortening
2 cups buttermilk

Mix yeast, sugar and hot tap water together and set aside.
Cut shortening into flour. Add yeast and sugar mixture and
buttermilk to the flour mixture. Mix only until flour is moist.
Knead dough twice. Pat dough to desired thickness, about
3/8 inch. Place in greased pan. Butter tops of biscuits with a
liquid butter. Bake 10-12 minutes in a 450 degree oven.
Makes about 45 biscuits, 2 1/4 inches in diameter.

JONESVILLE

Robert B. Winegeart
CATAHOULA PARISH

Dirt Cake

SERVES 12-15

1 1/4 lb. bag Oreo cookies, crushed
1/2 stick margarine
1 cup powdered sugar
8 oz. cream cheese
3 1/2 cups milk
2 packages instant vanilla pudding
   (small)
12 oz. Cool Whip

Mix together (last 6 ingredients) and layer with crushed Oreos. Hints: Make cake the night before serving. Keep refrigerated. Use your imagination with decorations. Makes a large amount, but will keep for several days. This is a fun cake and usually brings on the laughter. Just shovel the dirt in and enjoy every lump that goes into your mouth. "We put ours in a flower pot with cellophane and cover with a few "worms" (edible candy), topped with a silk flower.

JUNCTION CITY
Mrs. Margaret Templeton
UNION PARISH

Hot Rolls
SERVES 16-24

2 packages yeast
3 tbsp. warm water
2 eggs, beaten
1/2 cup sugar
1/2 cup shortening
1 tsp. salt
4 cups flour, sifted
1 cup warm water

Dissolve yeast in warm water and set aside. Mix eggs, sugar, shortening and salt well and stir in 1 cup warm water. Stir in yeast mixture and add 4 cups sifted flour - one cup at a time. Mix well (I use mixer). Cover bowl and place in refrigerator overnight. 2 to 3 hours before baking, roll to 1/2 inch thickness, spread with butter. Cut with biscuit cutter (any size). Place on buttered pan. Let rise 1 to 3 hours. Bake 6 minutes (maybe more) at 425 degrees. Very good.

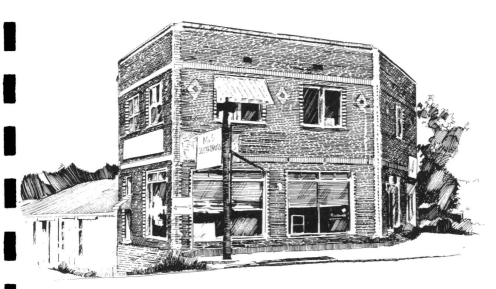

LAKE PROVIDENCE

Jeanette Clement
EAST CARROLL PARISH

Pound Cake
SERVES 10

8 eggs, separated
6 tbsp. sugar
1 lb. margarine
3 1/2 cups plain flour
1/2 cup light cream
2 3/4 cups sugar
1 tbsp. vanilla

Separate eggs and beat whites until stiff with 6 tbsp. sugar.
Cream margarine and sugar until well mixed. Add beaten egg
yolks. Add flour and cream alternately. Add vanilla. Fold in
stiffly beaten egg whites. Bake in large tube pan which has
been greased and floured at 350 degrees for 1 1/2 hours. Let
cool in pan 10 minutes before removing from pan.

MANGHAM

Annie W. Childress
RICHLAND PARISH

Seven Layer Delight

SERVES 8-10

Hamburger meat
1/2 cup onions, chopped
2 tubs Guacamole dip
1 can refried beans
Sour cream
Sliced olives
Cheddar cheese, shredded
Lettuce, chopped
Tomatoes, chopped
1 package Taco seasoning
Salt and pepper to taste

Brown hamburger meat with 1/2 cup chopped onions. Drain. Add taco seasoning. In serving dish layer, in order, refried beans, hamburger meat, guacamole dip, sour cream, chopped lettuce, tomatoes, and cheese. Add salsa if desired. Refrigerate 2 hours or overnight before serving.

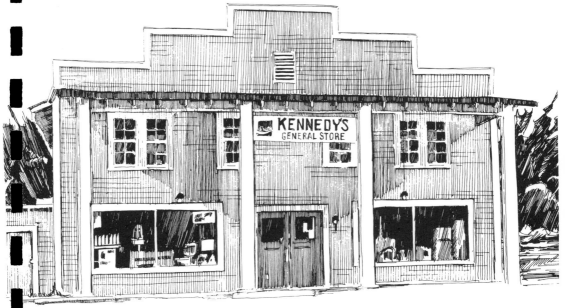

MARION
Lum Farr
UNION PARISH

Red Beans and Rice

SERVES 12

1 lb. red or pinto beans
1 medium onion, chopped
2 stalks celery, chopped
1 green pepper, chopped
1 lb. ham pieces
1 lb. smoked sausage
3 bay leaves
1 1/2 tsp. salt
1/2 tsp. red pepper
1 tsp. chili powder

Wash beans, soak in water overnight. Drain beans and place in large pot. Cut sausage into 1/2 inch pieces and brown in a little oil. Remove sausage and saute' onion, celery and green pepper in drippings. Add all ingredients to beans. Cover with water, bring to a boil, reduce heat and cook slowly until beans are tender. Serve over rice.

MER ROUGE

Jean Blackard
MOREHOUSE PARISH

Adrienne's Delight
SERVES 35

12 oz. Philadelphia Cream Cheese
1 stick butter
1/2 cup sugar
1/2 cup sour cream
1 envelope plain gelatin
1/4 cup cold water
1/2 cup white raisins
1 cup slivered almonds (toasted)
Grated rinds of 2 lemons
Saltine crackers
Small amount of lemon juice

Let cream cheese, butter and sour cream come to room temperature. Cream well, add sugar. Soften gelatin in 1/4 cup cold water - dissolve over hot water. Add to cream cheese mixture. Add raisins, almonds, lemon rind and juice. Grease 1 quart mold with butter. Put mixture in and refrigerate. When firm, unmold and serve with Saltine crackers. This can be used at cocktail parties or as a dessert with fruit. You can freeze this after unmolding. When ready to use - just thaw.

MONROE
Adrienne G. Smith
OUACHITA PARISH

Yum Yum Pineapple Salad

SERVES 12-14

2 cups crushed pineapple
1 cup sugar
Juice of 1 lemon
2 tbsp. gelatin
1 cup grated American
   cheese
1/2 cup cold water
1/2 pint whipping cream

Heat undrained pineapple: add juice and sugar and stir until dissolved. Soak gelatin in cold water 10 minutes; add to hot pineapple mixture and stir until dissolved. When it begins to set add cheese. Whip cream until stiff and fold into pineapple mixture; leave in mold until firm. Grease mold first with Wesson Oil. For dressing, mix 1/2 cup mayonnaise with 2 tbsp. finely chopped celery, 2 tbsp finely chopped bell pepper, 2 tbsp. finely chopped green onion and a few drops onion juice. For Christmas add 4 drops green food coloring in salad and top dressing with a red cherry.

MOUND

Elise C. Yerger
MADISON PARISH

Mandarin Orange Refrigerator Cake
SERVES 14-18

1 Duncan Hines Butter Cake Mix
4 eggs
3/4 cup oil
1 11 oz. can Mandarin Oranges
1 20 oz. can crushed pineapple
1 large package instant vanilla pudding
1 large container Cool Whip

Mix the cake mix, eggs, oil and the juice from the oranges. After mixed well, fold in the oranges so as not to mash them. Pour into 3 round 8" cake pans that have been sprayed with Pam and sprinkled with sugar. Bake at 350 degrees for 18-20 minutes. Cool before icing. ICING: Mix the pineapple and the juice with the pudding mix and the Cool Whip. Put between the layers and on top and sides of cake. Refrigerate overnight for better flavor.

NEWELLTON

Vicki Barfield
TENSAS PARISH

Sweet Potato Salad
SERVES 6

3 large sweet potatoes
4 hard boiled eggs, chopped
1 medium onion, chopped
1 cup celery, chopped
1 tsp. salt
1/8 tsp. pepper
1/4 cup salad dressing
1/4 cup Durkee's dressing

Mash sweet potatoes. Mix sweet potatoes, eggs, onions, celery, salt, pepper, salad dressing and Durkee's dressing. Refrigerate for at least 6 hours or overnight before serving.

OAK GROVE

Tami Bedenbender
WEST CARROLL PARISH

Caramel Pie

SERVES 6-8

2 cups milk
1 cup sugar
4 tbsp. flour
3 eggs, separated
1 tsp. vanilla
1 tbsp. butter

Put milk in heavy boiler over low heat. At the same time put
1/ 3 cup of the sugar in heavy aluminum boiler. Let melt over
low heat, stirring real often. In bowl mix rest of sugar, flour
and pinch of salt. Moisten with some of milk. Add egg yolks
and beat well. Add a little of hot milk. Then put sugar mixture
in milk. Cook until thickened, stirring constantly. The other
sugar should be melted by this time. Pour it into milk mixture
and stir until the caramelized sugar is well mixed. Turn off
heat. Add butter and vanilla. Beat egg whites adding 6 tbsp. of
sugar gradually for meringue. Beat until real stiff. Pour mixture
into baked pastry shell. Then add meringue. Bake in 350
degree oven for 15 minutes.

OAK RIDGE

Marion Files
MOREHOUSE PARISH

Chili-Cheese Balls
SERVES 6 DOZEN

2 cups shredded cheddar cheese
1 cup all-purpose flour
1/2 cup butter or margarine, softened
1/2 tsp. salt
1 can (4 ounce) chopped green chilies, well drained

Heat oven to 350 degrees. Mix all ingredients. Shape into 3/4 inch balls. Place about 2 inches apart on greased cookie sheet. Bake until set, 15 to 18 minutes. Serve immediately. Makes about 6 dozen appetizers of 30 calories each.

TIP: Shape and freeze. Bake 18 to 20 minutes.

OLLA
Carol McDougald
LA SALLE PARISH

Quick Enchiladas
SERVES 4 TO 6

1 package corn tortillas
2 cans chili (no beans)
1 large onion chopped fine
1 lb. sharp cheese, grated

Heat slightly the chili in a sauce pan larger than the tortilla. Dip each tortilla in the chili to soften and season. To each tortilla add 2 tbsp. cheese, 2 tbsp. onion and roll or fold inside. Place close together in 9" X 13" baking dish. Pour remaining chili over the top. Add more grated cheese if desired. Bake about 20 minutes or until onion is tender.

RAYVILLE

Juanita Cochran
RICHLAND PARISH

Rice Delicious
SERVES 6

1 stick butter
1 cup raw rice
1 can (med.) water chestnuts (reserve liquid)
1 can (med.) mushrooms (reserve liquid)
1 can onion soup

Melt butter. Saute' sliced mushrooms and water chestnuts in butter. Add cup of onion soup. Pour reserved liquids into empty soup can and finish filling with water. Pour cup of rice into casserole. Add mixture and stir. Bake in preheated 300 degree oven for 1 hour in covered casserole.
Serve with all types of barbecue, roast pork or steak.

SICILY ISLAND

Sue Peace
CATAHOULA PARISH

Mexican Corn Bread
SERVES 6 TO 8

1 1/2 cups corn meal
1 cup cream style corn
1 cup sour cream
2/3 cup salad oil
2 eggs
3 tsp. baking powder
1 tsp. salt
2 jalapeno peppers
(chopped)
1 1/2 cups sharp cheese

Mix ingredients in order listed. Do not mix cheese. Pour half of mixture in hot greased 10 1/2 inch iron skillet. Sprinkle 1/2 cheese over this and add remaining mix. Cover with cheese and bake at 350 degrees for 40 - 45 minutes. (Very good on New Years Day with black eye peas and cabbage.)

SONDHEIMER

Wanda Oliver
EAST CARROLL PARISH

Pecan Pie
SERVES 6

1/2 cup of sugar
2 eggs
1 cup of chopped pecans
2 tbsp. corn meal
1 cup dark Karo syrup

Combine and bake slowly in an unbaked pie shell.

ST. JOSEPH

Byron Temple
TENSAS PARISH

Pineapple-Beef Kabobs
SERVES 8 TO 10

2 (20-ounce) cans pineapple chunks, undrained
1/2 cup firmly packed brown sugar
2/3 cup cider vinegar
2/3 cup catsup
1/4 cup soy sauce
2 tsp. ground ginger
1 1/2 tsp. liquid smoke
3 pounds boneless sirloin tip roast, cut into 1 1/2 inch
cubes (Kabobs)
1/2 pound fresh mushroom caps
2 small onions, quartered
2 medium size green peppers, cut into 1 inch pieces

Drain pineapple, reserving juice. Combine pineapple juice
and next 6 ingredients, mixing well; pour into a large shallow
dish. Add meat; cover and marinate overnight in refrigerator.
Drain meat, reserving marinade. Pour marinade in a saucepan; bring to a boil. Add mushrooms; reduce heat and simmer, uncovered, 10 minutes. Drain, reserving marinade. Set
mushrooms aside. Alternate meat, pineapple chunks, mushrooms, onion, and green pepper on 8 to 10 skewers. Grill
kabobs over medium-hot coals 10 to 15 minutes or until
desired degree of doneness, brushing frequently with marinade. Serve the kabobs with rice.

TALLULAH
Jack Millikin
MADISON PARISH

Pork Roast

SERVES 6

3 to 4 lb. pork loin
Straight link of pork sausage (Hillshire's)
2 tbsp. Worcestershire powder
1 tsp. salt
2 tsp. black pepper
1/4 tsp. ground ginger
1/4 green pepper

Freeze pork sausage. Use a long butcher knife and cut an X thru the roast from end to end and stuff the frozen sausage thru the roast. Rub roast down with seasonings. Cut slits in the roast and stuff pieces of green pepper. Bake at 325 degrees for 2 hours in an open pan. Very tasty and pretty on a plate.

TRANSYLVANIA

Pat Fairchild
EAST CARROLL PARISH

"Chocolate Squares" Cake
SERVES 8

2 cups plain flour
2 cups sugar
3 tbsp. cocoa
1 tsp. soda
1 tsp. vanilla
1/2 tsp. salt
1 stick oleo
1/2 cup shortening
2 eggs
1/2 cup buttermilk
1 cup water

ICING:
1 stick oleo
3 tbsp. cocoa
1 tsp. vanilla
6 tbsp. milk
1 box powdered sugar
1 cup chopped nuts (pecans)
3 tbsp. peanut butter

In large bowl mix flour, sugar and salt. In saucepan mix oleo, water, shortening and cocoa and bring to a boil. Pour over flour mixture. In a small bowl mix eggs, soda, buttermilk and vanilla together. Add to the first mixture. Bake in a large sheet pan which has been greased and floured. Bake at 350 degrees for 25 to 30 minutes. ICING: Combine oleo, milk, and cocoa and melt, but do not boil.   Turn off heat. Add remaining ingredients and stir well. Pour on cake while it is still hot.

TULLOS

Mrs. Fred Book
LA SALLE PARISH

Hamburger Casserole

SERVES 6

1 lb. hamburger
1 can Rotel tomatoes
1 can cream mushroom soup
1 can cream celery soup
1 bag Doritoes
6 slices American cheese
Salt to taste
Pepper to taste

Brown hamburger meat and seasonings. Combine and beat thoroughly Rotel tomatoes, mushroom soup and cream celery soup. Place Doritoes in casserole dish, put in browned hamburger on top of Doritoes. Add 3 slices cheese on top of hamburger then pour soup mixtures over all ingredients. Put 3 slices of cheese on top of mixture, cover with foil and bake at 350 degrees for about 30-45 min. (Until cheese is melted)

URANIA

Jodie K. Ganey
LA SALLE PARISH

Southern Peach Cobbler
SERVES 12

FILLING:
2 (29 oz.) cans sliced peaches
(drain and reserve juice)
1 1/2 cup sugar
3 or 4 tbsp. cornstarch
2 sticks melted margarine
(add 1 stick to pie mixture,
reserve 1 stick to pour on the
top crust)
1/2 tsp. nutmeg
(add to pie filling)

PIE CRUST:
2 cups flour
1/2 tsp. salt
2/3 cup shortening
5 or 6 tbsp. ice water

Mix all the pie filling ingredients together and if it seems too
thick, add a small amount of the juice. Pour in a 9" X 13" pan
that has been lined with a thin crust. Place a crust on top and
fold extra dough over pie. Melt 1 stick of margarine and brush
over top. Sprinkle 1/4 cup sugar on top. Bake at 325 degrees
for approximately 1 hour or until golden brown.
PIE CRUST: Mix flour, salt and shortening together until the
size of peas. Add water until dough holds together but not
tough. Divide into 2 equal parts.

VIDALIA
Fay Garretson
CONCORDIA PARISH

Squash Casserole

SERVES 4

2 cups cooked squash
2 cups cooked corn bread
2 eggs
1/4 stick oleo
1 small jar pimento
1 small onion, chopped
1 can cream of chicken soup
Salt and pepper to taste

Mix all ingredients together in 2 quart ovenproof dish and bake at 350 degrees until bubbly hot. This dish can also be cooked in a microwave.

WATERPROOF

Beverly Rushing
TENSAS PARISH

Dirty Rice
SERVES 4

1 lb. hot bulk pork sausage
2 bunches green onions, chopped
1 medium white onion, chopped
1/1/2 cups long grain rice, uncooked
3 cups water
Salt
Pepper
Tony's Creole Seasoning

In cast iron skillet brown sausage and onions with seasonings, drain all but 2 tbsp. fat from skillet, add rice and water. Bring to boil. Turn down heat and simmer 15 minutes or until rice is tender.

WEST MONROE

Betsy Ross
OUACHITA PARISH

Ramage's Ribs

SERVES SEVERAL

Ribs
2 or 3 large onions
1 cup oil
1 cup vinegar
1 cup pineapple juice
1 or 2 lemons (sliced)
8-10 cloves garlic
1 cup Lea & Perrins
1/2 can of beer
Salt and pepper

Place ribs over a slow cooking, smoky charcoal fire. Mesquite or pecan chips may be added for flavor. Prepare basting sauce by saute'ing onions and garlic in some of the oil. When tender add remaining oil and other ingredients and simmer. Use basting sauce on ribs for the first 2 hours. Baste often so that almost all of the liquid is gone. TABLE SAUCE: 1 small can crushed pineapple and 1 bottle (about a quart) commercial BBQ sauce. Use the onions, garlic and lemons left as the base for the table sauce. Add about a quart of good commercial BBQ sauce and small can of crushed pineapple and simmer. Salt and pepper to taste. Use this sauce for 30 to 60 minutes of cooking and also at the table. Total cooking time is about 3 hours.

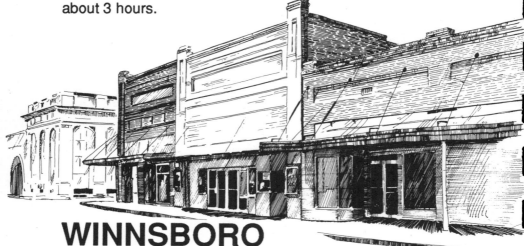

WINNSBORO

John R. Adams
FRANKLIN PARISH

Vegetable Casserole
SERVES 6

1 can shoe peg corn
1 can French style beans
1 can celery soup
1 can water chestnuts
1/2 cup diced celery
1/2 cup onions
1/2 cup sharp cheese
1/2 cup sour cream (or more)
1/4 cup diced bell pepper

Put in large casserole dish and dot with 1/2 stick oleo. Put
Ritz crackers or Cheese Nip crumbs on top. Bake at 350
degrees for 45 minutes.

WISNER

Mrs. Sue Kiper
FRANKLIN PARISH

LOUISIANA COOKING TERMS

Much of the cooking in Louisiana is unique to the State. Also unique are some of the terms which apply to the ingredients or recipes. Some of the words used in the book are noted here, along with a brief definition.

ANDOUILLE
Cajun pure pork, highly seasoned smoked sausage.

COURTBOUILLON
Thick stew or soup made of fish and served over rice.

CRACKLING
Crisp fried pork skin.

ETOUFFEE
Smothered shrimp or crawfish and chopped vegetables.

FILE'
Powdered sassafras tree leaves used as a flavoring, usually on gumbo's.

GUMBO
Soup like mixture made with a roux and several types of meats or seafood and served over rice.

JAMBALAYA
Mixture of different meats, seafood or poultry and vegetables and rice. Usually highly seasoned.

ROUX
Equal parts flour and oil cooked until very brown. Is used as the base for a lot of Louisiana dishes.

SAUCE PIQUANTE
Thick mixture (sauce) of roux and tomatoes, highly seasoned and cooked low for hours.

TOWN INDEX

299

RECIPE INDEX

BREAD

DESSERTS

DRESSING

GUMBO AND SOUP

JAMBALAYA

MEAT

POULTRY

SALAD

SEAFOOD

VEGETABLES

303

Please send _____ copies of the Louisiana Proud
Collection of Home Cooking at $12.95 per copy. (Postage for
1 book is $1.75. Add $.25 for each additional copy.)

NAME _____

ADDRESS_____

CITY _____ STATE _____ ZIP _____

_____ Please send a Louisiana Proud Product Brochure.

Louisiana Proud
6133 Goodwood Ave.   Baton Rouge, La. 70806

Please send _____ copies of the Louisiana Proud
Collection of Home Cooking at $12.95 per copy. (Postage for
1 book is $1.75. Add $.25 for each additional copy.)

NAME _____

ADDRESS_____

CITY _____ STATE _____ ZIP _____

_____ Please send a Louisiana Proud Product Brochure.

Louisiana Proud
6133 Goodwood Ave.   Baton Rouge, La. 70806